10
Easy Ways
to Use
Technology in the
English Classroom

10 Easy Ways

to Use

Technology in the

English Classroom

Hilve Firek Foreword by **Jeffrey D. Wilhelm**

HEINEMANN ● Portsmouth, NH

Heinemann
A division of Reed Elsevier Inc.
361 Hanover Street
Portsmouth, NH 03801–3912
www.heinemann.com

Offices and agents throughout the world

The author and publisher wish to thank those who have generously given permission to reprint borrowed material:

Clip art is from *www.clipart.com.* Copyright © 2003 *www.clipart.com.*

Figure 9–1 is used by permission of Advanced Learning Technologies, University of Kansas. Copyright © 1995–2002 by ALTec.

Images in Figures 10–1 and 10–2 are from istockphoto.com.

Library of Congress Cataloging-in-Publication Data
Firek, Hilve.
   Ten easy ways to use technology in the English classroom / Hilve Firek.
     p. cm.
   ISBN 0-325-00547-8
     1. English philology—Study and teaching—Technological innovations.
   2. Educational technology. I. Title : 10 easy ways to use technology in the English classroom. II. Title.

   PE66.F57 2004
   428'.0071—dc21   2003050918

Editor: Lisa Luedeke
Production service: bookworks, Lisa S. Garboski
Production coordinator: Sonja S. Chapman
Cover design: Night & Day Design
Compositor: Drawing Board Studios/Valerie Levy
Manufacturing: Steve Bernier

Printed in the United States of America on acid-free paper
09   08   07   06   05   VP   2   3   4   5

Contents

Foreword

by Jeffrey D. Wilhelm

Hilve Firek has written an important and much needed contribution to the English and language arts teaching profession with *Ten Easy Ways to Use Technology in the English Classroom*. Technological facility is essential to literacy in the twenty-first century and yet few teachers truly use technology themselves or teach and assist students to learn how to use technologies for various literate purposes.

In Deborah Brandt's Grawemeyer award–winning book, *Literacy in American Lives* (2002), the author traces how the literate demands of our personal, educational, and professional lives have increased exponentially over the past century due, in large part, to the cultural uses of electronic technologies. In personal conversation, Brandt—a highly distinguished and perhaps our foremost historian of literacy—confided to me that she used to think "technology had little to do with literacy. Now I know that technology has everything to do with literacy, and literacy has everything to do with technology."

I agree. Being literate has always meant the ability to create and communicate meaning with the most powerful cultural tools available. These tools are now electronic. As Jay David Bolter, a Professor of Language, Communication, and Culture at the Georgia Institute of Technology, argues in his seminal work *The Writing Space* (1991), students who do not read and compose multimedia can truly be considered "illiterate" today, since these are the tools of the Internet and the basis for much electronic communication.

Yet the past twenty-one years of my own experience working in schools, and various reviews of American teaching, lead me to believe that many language arts and English teachers are reluctant to integrate technology into their classrooms.

Some teachers may not believe technological literacies are important or are not related to our primary concerns as English teachers—a position I believe to be untenable—and that Hilve Firek deftly and considerately shows to be untrue.

Some teachers may be uncomfortable with their own lack—or relative lack (compared to students, anyway!)—of technological expertise. Others may see technology as an add-on, as something extra to do in an already too crowded curriculum.

Some may not see how technological applications will help students to meet the demands of reading and writing literature, or meet the demands of literary reading, or of today's standards and tests.

To all these folks, I would say two things: First, I would invoke Ron Passman's eloquent injunction that "Good teaching always overcomes bad testing." Second, I would advise: read Hilve Firek.

Hilve Firek's powerful and informative book deftly addresses these concerns. She shows that we can easily learn to use various accessible technologies in the classroom, and learn to use them more effectively. She shows how we can use technologies to motivate and engage learners and to better achieve the cultural ends we have always so rightly cared about: assisting kids to be better readers, writers, thinkers, and democratic citiizens. She provides many smart, situated ways to deal with real teaching issues with greater success. She shows how practicing teachers can layer and adapt audio, video, hypermedia, and other applications into our current practices to transform teaching and learning without causing us any extra work. In fact, she shows how using technology as a tool can make things simpler as it motivates students and extends their and our own abilities to work. It's brilliant stuff as she shows how to promote substantive literacy learning by embedding technological design projects in the context of what most of us are *already* trying to do.

This is a very rich and practical book, but its richness goes beyond its profoundly useful practical implications. In fact, I perceived many powerful themes carefully interwoven implicitly between these pages. I'd like to mention just three of them that particularly resonated with me as a thinker, theorist, researcher, and always as a teacher.

First, the core of this book is about democratic teaching. Throughout we see the importance of valuing and using students' home resources as a way of expanding our notions of literacy and of bridging students from what they know and value to what they can know and become next with our careful assistance. The book draws on multiple intelligences and repeatedly demonstrates the importance of seeing various perspectives and representing what we know in various ways and media. The work here celebrates and draws on the importance of working in a community of learners and inquirers. Firek's work especially addresses the needs of our most struggling students and finds ways of inviting them in to this community.

Second, this book maps on to the most current research about student motivation and engagement. When Michael Smith and I recently researched the literate lives of adolescent boys (*Reading Don't Fix No Chevys*, 2002) we isolated several important findings that resound throughout Hilve Firek's book. Primary of these is the importance of a social purpose for all learning, since purpose drives your motivation, what you attend to, and what you will remember. Another is the need for teachers to provide contextualized assistance that helps students to do their "own work" versus "playing guess what the teacher already knows," as one of our informants put it. We also found that the boys in our study all valued and used technology in their own lives (this included even the students from the most impoverished circumstances) and were cynical about how school literacy did not match the literacy they experienced and perceived in lives outside of school. For our boys, technology exhibited what Sherry Turkle calls "holding power."

Finally, this book exemplifies, through its rich models and descriptions of classroom practice and implementations, the theory of constructivist "learning centered teaching" (Wilhelm, Baker, and Dube, 2001) that recent research in cognitive psychology supports so strongly. This book opens the door to the use of inquiry and design projects, of teacher research (as teachers use student-designed artifacts to make student thinking visible and transparent so that their teaching can be more informed and appropriate), and of instruction that uses technology to assist students to grow and develop competence and confidence as literate beings. Through all this work, students are helped to see the power of technology to promote literacy and literate work, and to develop independence as people who can articulate and apply their own critical standards—certainly a bulwark of democratic culture that is too rarely promoted in schools.

And I can't help saying that the book is well written, with humor and the authority of classroom practice, and fun to read—even if one is tired and reading for a half hour before bedtime. I can't think of a reason not to read this book; I have to think that it will seep into your teaching mind and positively affect the way you think and practice as a teacher of literacy.

Works Cited

Bolter, J. D. 1991. *Writing Space.*

Brandt, Deborah. 2001. *Literacy in American Lives.* NY: Cambridge UP.

Smith, Michael and Jeffery Wilhelm. 2002. *Reading Don't Fix No Chevys.* Portsmouth, NH: Heinemann.

Wilhelm, Jeffery, Tanya Baker, and Julie Dube. 2001. *Strategic Reading.* Portsmouth, NH: Heinemann.

Acknowledgments

I wish first to thank my editor, Lisa Luedeke, for her infinite patience and insightful suggestions. Most of all, I want to express my sincere gratitude for her confidence and support in this project.

Next, I must thank Beverly Ann Chin. She took me by the hand when I needed it, and she directed my professional growth in ways I did not know were possible. She is an incredible mentor and a true friend.

I say thank you as well to the professors at the University of Montana who guided my thinking and challenged my preconceptions: David Erickson, Sally Brewer, Lisa Blank, Len Foster, Stephanie Wasta, and Carolyn Lott.

My thanks also go out to the English student teachers who participated in our online-community pilot: Brittanny Black, Keith Grebetz, Violet Hopkins, Eric Law, Meghann Shrader, and Frank White. I learned so much from each of them.

And I extend my gratitude to those colleagues who have encouraged me through the years: Denny Wolfe, Bob Probst, Kathleen Bell, Corey Lock, Gene Schaffer, Elaine Simos, Jan Andrejco, Jim Rayfield, and Steve Purcell.

Thank you to Chris Martineau, Steve Tull, and all the teachers at Superior High School in Superior, Montana. The work we did with Writing Across the Curriculum contributed to many of the ideas in this book.

The words "thank you" do not begin to express my heartfelt gratitude for my dear friend Martha Cheney. Her support was unwavering, her shoulder was strong, and her front porch was inviting.

And of course, to my husband Bob: Thank you.

Introduction

Can't you just teach me something I can use in my classroom tomorrow?

This is the plea I heard over and over from middle- and high-school English teachers enrolled in my "Technology in the Classroom" courses at Roosevelt University in suburban Chicago. *Ten Easy Ways to Use Technology in the English Classroom* is a response to that plea.

As lovers of language, literature, and writing, English teachers are sometimes daunted by the prospect of integrating technology into teaching. *Ten Easy Ways to use Technology in the English Classroom* will show you how to incorporate a variety of technologies—computers, camcorders, even television—into the lessons you are already teaching. The book includes simple, step-by-step examples so you can implement new ideas quickly. I have created a companion website (www.teneasyways.com) so you can download project templates, access resources, and communicate with others who are trying the ideas in this book. When you see the computer icon in this book, go to this website for additional resources.

Too often, professors of instructional technology focus too heavily on the machinery, not on the day-to-day realities of teaching. *Ten Easy Ways to Use Technology in the English Classroom* will take the mystery out of technology by offering teachers easy-to-follow examples of projects that can be incorporated into preexisting lessons.

As we all know, states are increasingly asking teachers of all content areas to integrate technology into their instruction, as evidenced by published standards. *Ten Easy Ways to Use Technology in the English Classroom* will help you meet the Standards for the English Language Arts outlined by the National Council of Teachers of English (NCTE) and the International Reading Association (IRA); correlations to state standards are on the companion website.

How the Book Is Organized

Ten Easy Ways to Use Technology in the English Classroom begins with projects that ask you to take a fresh look at ways to meaningfully integrate technologies you are already familiar with: audio, video, television, and movies. It then moves into the realm of computers. In the computer chapters I again begin with those technologies you are likely familiar with: email and word processing. The book then works its way through the perhaps unknown territory of concept mapping software, websites, and presentation packages.

Each chapter includes an interview with a teacher who uses technology to enhance language-arts instruction, margin links to online resources, and rubrics for assessing student learning.

As you try the projects in this book, access the companion website to discuss with other teachers what you and your students do in *your* classroom. Post your ideas on the discussion boards, and access regularly updated links to resources mentioned in *Ten Easy Ways to Use Technology in the English Classroom*. The goal of this book is to help you integrate technology into your daily teaching life in meaningful ways that create even more opportunities for you and your students to grown and learn.

1

Listening to and Creating Audio Theater

I freely admit that I'm an audio junkie. My husband and I recently took a drive cross-country, and we listened to the David Sedaris box set almost the entire way. There's something uniquely enjoyable about listening to what industry experts now call "audio theater."

Audio theater encompasses everything from books-on-tape to radio plays to audio documentaries for the Web. And people are listening. According to the Audio Publishers' Association, Americans spent a whopping $1.6 billion on audiobooks in 1996 alone (Fish 1999). And it's not just us old folks who have rediscovered the spoken word. The rhyme and rhythm of hip-hop has enticed an entire generation to fall in love with the music of words. Poetry slams have taken the nation's cities by storm, and organizations like Youth Speaks in San Francisco work to nurture and grow the voices of the young.

Adding to this growing interest are advances in technology that offer us the opportunity to access and create audio faster and cheaper than ever before. For example, sound can now be completely mobile. You can download every song ever recorded by The Beatles onto an MP3 player that fits in your pocket. And you no longer need expensive studio equipment to produce high-quality audio theater. GoldWave, an easy-to-use sound editor, can be downloaded to your PC for around $40, and you can find a number of free sound editors by searching a central site such as CNet. Of course, Windows bundles a simple sound recorder with its accessories; all you may need is an external microphone.

But creating meaningful learning experiences with audio theater doesn't require *any* computer equipment. If you don't have access to a PC in your classroom—or if you can't get time in your school's computer lab—then good old-fashioned tape recorders will do just fine. After all, it's not the quality of the *product* that's important; it's the *process* of learning through sound.

Listening to Learn

With so much emphasis on technology's appeal to the visual learner, we sometimes forget that some students need to *listen* to learn. They need the experience of hearing, processing, and *imagining*. Listening to, designing, and creating their own audio theater can provide that experience. Consider, for example, the learning that takes place when students create audio documentaries that explore, in depth, issues pertinent to their lives. To produce a documentary on, say, the implications of high-stakes testing, students would need to decide on interview subjects, conduct research, devise questions that strike to the heart of the issue, evaluate the quality of responses, select sound bites that tell the story, add music, and insert commentary. Each of the above tasks requires students to work together, to make evaluative decisions, and to *create*.

Another popular choice for audio theater is radio plays: Students create radio stories—complete with music and sound effects—to accompany the literature they're reading in class. In essence, almost any endeavor in an English class can be transferred to audio.

These projects help young people become better and more descriptive writers as they learn to "see" with their ears. They can also help focus student attention to the essential skill of *listening*, a skill sometimes overlooked in the curriculum. Perhaps most importantly, asking students to create media has been shown to be quite effective in helping students acquire new knowledge, build basic skills, and reflect on their learning (Simkins 2002, 8).

Of course, to create a successful piece of audio theater, your students must engage in those practices near and dear to English teachers' hearts: reading, writing, speaking, and listening. As with all the technology projects in this book, the audio theater tasks don't require you to add anything to your curriculum; you're just approaching your curriculum from another angle. In fact, you will notice that the steps of creating audio theater look conspicuously like the steps of the writing process.

2

Step 1: Listen Up!

If you and your students are not familiar with the many styles of audio theater, you might want to start your audio journey on the Web. Luckily, free audio abounds on the Internet. The type of players required for free audio varies, but if you have Windows Media Player and Real Player installed, you'll be able to hear most it. (To download the free Windows Media Player, go to windowsmedia.com; to download Real Player, go to real.com and find the link to the free player. Also, most sites that offer audio include links to download the necessary players.)

If you are unable to do this, National Public Radio (NPR) provides wonderful examples of a variety of audio works in its daily programs. Tape them yourselves or write to NPR to receive audio versions of their shows. You can also browse their many program selections at npr.org.

Once your media players are installed, you can begin your audio adventure. Tell your students that they are going to hear a variety of audio works—some documentaries, some works of fiction. Because they will eventually create their own piece of audio theater, they should try to determine what makes a piece engaging. Is it the people's voices? Is it the accompanying music? The listening guide in Figure 1–1 is available in a printable format on the companion website. Adapt it to help your students listen attentively.

Particularly rich and engaging is National Public Radio's *Lost and Found Sound*, a collection of radio stories, documentaries, and "audio artifacts." You can choose from any number of interesting pieces, but I think you will find the September 11 memorial, a collection of sounds and stories, especially stirring. The creators of *Lost and Found Sound* describe their "sonic memorial" in these words:

> We came together over the last year—a national collaboration of radio producers, artists, iron workers, bond traders, historians, widows and widowers, public radio listeners—to chronicle and commemorate the life and history of the World Trade Center and its neighborhood. We set up a phone line, and hundreds of you left your testimony and remembrances, poems, music, on-site recordings, small shards of sound. From this collection, and from dozens of interviews done by producers across the nation, the Sonic Memorial Project has created "A September Story," an intimate and historic radio documentary marking the anniversary of 9/11.

Also available on the *Lost and Found Sound* website is "Voices from the Dustbowl," a collection of audio recordings chronicling those who left the plains and headed for the promised land of California. Of course, this listening experience would be an excellent supplement to a study of *The Grapes of Wrath* or Karen Hesse's *Out of the Dust*:

> In 1940 two sound recordists, Charles Todd and Robert Sonkin, traveled to the California central valley—the flat, agricultural land that Steinbeck wrote about in

Listening Guide		
Prelistening	Title of program:	
	Purpose:	
	Type of program (talk show, documentary, radio play, other):	
	What I'm expecting is:	
Listening	The first thing I notice about this program is:	
	What I notice about the voices I'm hearing is:	
	What I notice about the music I'm hearing is:	
	What I notice about the story is:	
Post listening	My overall impression of the audio work is:	
	If I were going to produce a similar piece, I would:	
	I think they needed access to this equipment:	
	If I were going to produce a similar piece, I would need access to:	
	Other comments:	

Figure 1–1

The Grapes of Wrath. There, hundreds of refugees from Arkansas and Oklahoma had gathered—an exodus from their drought ridden and Depression ravaged home-lands. Dispatched by the Library of Congress, Todd and Sonkin set off to create an audio oral history of the lives of these Dust Bowl refugees.... The sounds of their new lives—the storytelling, love ballads, debates and square dance calls of a people in transit—were captured in these evocative recordings by Todd, Sonkin, and a fifty pound "Presto" disc recorder.

You'll find similar outstanding audio programs on most of the NPR program-ming links. A few examples: *American RadioWorks* features documentaries and in-vestigative reports. On its site you'll find a documentary on American life in the South under Jim Crow. Follow the links to find RealAudio interviews from both blacks and whites who lived "behind the veil." If you would prefer radio documentaries that focus on the environment, check out *Living on Earth*. If you want to take your students on an aural journey to the far reaches of the globe, then *Radio Expeditions* is the show for you.

Another great place for finding audio theater is the American Memory site from the Library of Congress. Go to memory.loc.gov and use their "collection finder" to search specifically for sound recordings. You'll find music from the Omaha Indians, "man-on-the-street" interviews following the Pearl Harbor attacks, presidential inauguration speeches, early sound recordings by Thomas Edison, and much more.

In addition to completing the listening guide, ask your students to respond—in writing and conversation—to what they hear. Guide them in analyzing the effectiveness of the radio stories. Were they engaging? If so, why? If not, why? Were they too long or too short? What was the impact of "audio artifacts," the voices of the people who were there? How did the voices of "real people," complete with slang and dialect, contribute to the story? Did the story elicit an emotional response? Why or why not?

By attending to audio theater, your students will begin to learn how words and sounds combine to create an overall effect for the listener. Further, they will start to see how the knowledge and skills they are acquiring in their English classes may be applied to the world beyond school.

Step 2: Plan (What Else?)

Now that you and your students are familiar with some of the facets of audio theater, you can begin planning your own projects. Ask your students to brainstorm ideas for their audio theater. The chart shown in Figure 1–2 is available in a printable format on the companion website. Adapt it as you wish. The chart is meant to help your students as they begin thinking about audio theater. Many more categories and examples exist.

Once they have decided on a topic for their audio theater, your students need to consider roles, tasks, equipment, and timelines. So that everyone has an opportunity to actively participate, many teachers break students into groups of three or four for audio theater projects. Also, consider telling students to limit their finished project to no more than ten or fifteen minutes. Usually, anything longer becomes unwieldy to manage and tedious to listen to.

Adapt the chart in Figure 1–3—available on the companion website—to meet your students' unique needs. Roles, of course, can be combined or assumed by the team as a whole, and the only equipment you really need is a tape recorder and some blank cassettes, though your students may enjoy experimenting with your computer's sound recording accessories.

Audio Theater Project Ideas		
Type of Audio Theater	Example	Your Ideas
Nonfiction documentary	The implications of high-stakes testing on our school and community	
Creative nonfiction	An afternoon at the community center	
Creative fiction	Poetry slams	
Adapted fiction	A section from *The Giver* as a radio play	
News programming	Sports update	
Quiz show	Unit review as a game show (à la NPR's *Wait, Wait, Don't Tell Me*)	
Other		

Figure 1–2

Step 3: Conduct Research

Careful research is essential to audio theater. For example, if your students are creating a documentary about your district's dropout rate, they need to find accurate statistics and demographic information. But they also need to conduct research to discover the *human* side of the story. They need to find out what really happens to students who drop out of school. They need to determine the best people to talk with in order to present a story that has impact and includes a number of different viewpoints. They need to find people whose *voices* tell the real story.

Step 4: Create

Once students identify the people to best tell the story, they need to schedule and conduct interviews. If time is short—and it always is—consider asking your students to limit their interviews to people at school. To continue with the earlier example about dropouts, students could interview a principal, a teacher, a student whose brother or sister quit school, and someone who is considering quitting school. For mobility, have your students conduct their interviews on old-fashioned tape recorders. If they wish, they can upload the recordings for editing on their computers later.

Audio Theater Planning Guide	
Type of production (creative nonfiction, adapted fiction, etc.):	
Working title:	
Roles	
Narrator(s):	
Interviewer(s):	
Sound technician(s):	
Researcher(s):	
Writer(s):	
Equipment needed (microphone, tape recorder, cassettes, computer sound editor, music CDs, etc.):	
Project timeline	
Day 1	Meet to decide topic and roles; review assessment criteria
Day 2	Outline or create graphic organizer for story
Day 3	Research
Day 4	Research
Day 5	Record interviews
Day 6	Log media elements and decide on "gems"
Day 7	Write and record narration; select music
Day 8	Mix interviews; add music and narration
Day 9	Present audio theater to classmates; complete self-reflection

© 2003 by Hilve Firek from *Ten Easy Ways to Use Technology in the English Classroom*. Portsmouth, NH: Heinemann.

Figure 1–3

Once groups have conducted their interviews, they need to sit down to-gether and listen for "gems," the nuggets of sound that capture the essence of their story. They also need to keep a log of their interviews—who says what and when—so they can find what they're looking for when it comes time to mix. If they are using tape recorders that don't have counters, they can log their inter-views using a stopwatch or even a watch with a second hand. The log sheet in Figure 1–4 may help your students as they chronicle their interviews. You can download a printable version of the form on this book's companion website.

Sample Interview Log			
Tape Number	In Time	Out Time	Comments
1	00:00:00	00:01:20	Brief interview with Nathan. His brother dropped out. He comments that "He's 18, and it's his life." Might be good as a sound bite in the introduction.
1	00:01:32	00:08:02	Interview with Ms. Wilson, the senior English teacher. She talks about how "education enriches the individual." Maybe use in the ending?

Figure 1–4

Use this form to help you keep track of your interviews. If your equipment doesn't have a counter, use a stopwatch to note where on the tape an interview is located.

In the sample shown, the first interview is found at the beginning of the tape, and it ends 1 minute and 20 seconds later. The second interview logged is found 1 minute and 32 seconds into the tape and it ends 6 minutes and 30 seconds later.

Next, students need to write and record narration. To write the commentary, students should consider what they need to say in order to "set the stage." Remind them that the voices of their interviewees should tell the story. Narration is generally used only for introductions and transitions.

Similarly, when selecting music, students should consider the tone of their audio theater, and choose music appropriately. In essence, music should add to the emotional nature of the piece, not detract from it.

Step 5: Mix, Edit, and Produce

When it comes to mixing, remind students that simple is best. Award-winning audio theater often consists of only one or two voices and a smidgeon of music.

To mix a final tape, all you really need is two tape recorders, a microphone, the cassettes with the interviews, narration, and music, a blank cassette, and a quiet room. Students play the sound clips and music in the order they want on one tape player while recording them on the other. The finished product might not be ready for radio, but the *process* of producing authentic radio theater helps students hone their reading, writing, speaking, and listening skills. Perhaps most important, they begin to see the real value of effective and concise communication in the world beyond the classroom walls.

If your students want to experiment with sound-editing software, they can record their interviews, music, and narration simply by using a computer microphone and the sound recorder that comes with Windows. Or they can connect their recording devices to the computer and record from the line-in. Because computer sound editors vary greatly, students will need to check individual read-me files for instructions.

Step 6: Share and Distribute

Of course, no theater project would be complete without a production. Have students share their work with one another and with the people they interviewed. Consider making a master tape for your school's library, and send a copy to your local public radio station. Who knows? Maybe they'll air a segment or two....

Assessment Checklist

Authentic learning often resists traditional assessment, but the checklist in Figure 1–5 may help guide your students in their work. Access the printable form on the companion website.

9

✓	Audio Theater Project Checklist
	Audio
	Selected audio is consistent with the type of theater produced.
	All audio clips contribute to the overall theme or message.
	Music is appropriate for the theme.
	Final product plays consistently and is free of technical bugs.
	Research, writing, and language use
	Research was thorough; information is accurate.
	Narration is clear and concise.
	Language in narration is free of structural or grammatical errors.
	Collaboration
	Each person in the group completed assigned tasks completely and on time.
	Each person contributed to the overall learning of the group.
	Each person participated in a positive manner.

Figure 1–5

Reflection

Taking time to reflect is an essential part of learning. Reflective contemplation helps us process our thoughts and put our learning into perspective. Ask your students to consider what they've learned by responding to the project in their journals, or adapt the following handout in Figure 1–6, available in a printable format on the companion website.

In essence, producing audio theater helps students make a real connection to the spoken word. They learn to listen critically by attending to the blending of words and sounds. Most important, they begin to recognize that the language-arts activities they partake in at school really do have purposes beyond the end-of-course test.

This Corvallis Life

Charlyn Ellis is an English teacher at Corvallis High School in Corvallis, Oregon, a medium-sized town in the Willamette Valley. When I called her to chat about the audio theater her seniors produce, she laughed.

"This is for a technology book?" she asked. "That is so funny because I'm like a Luddite. I can't even operate the VCR."

But lack of expertise in the latest bells and whistles doesn't keep Ellis from having her students participate in meaningful learning experiences by writing and producing radio stories.

Audio Theater Reflection

Before this project, this is what I knew about audio theater:

My group created this type of program:

Before we started I expected...

After we began working, I noticed...

What I enjoyed most about the project:

What I enjoyed least about the project:

What I learned about our topic:

What I learned about the research process:

What I learned about interviewing:

What I learned about writing:

What I learned about working in a group:

My overall impression of our audio work:

If I were going to do this project again, I would...

Other comments:

Figure 1–6

Ellis explained that she was inspired by the National Public Radio show *This American Life,* produced by host Ira Glass.

"Honestly, I worship the ground Ira Glass walks on," she said. "He captures the essence of what's going on in America. He's got a knack for finding the story that's worth finding. And I love how there's a theme that runs through each segment."

Ellis has her seniors create their own radio stories—stories collectively titled *This Corvallis Life.*

"What I want them to be able to do as writers is to create vignettes, brief essential experiences," she said, "you know, the kind that are based on David James Duncan's idea of the river tooth . . ., those essential moments that tell a story. I've got thirty four kids in the room, and I can't read five-page papers every week, so I'm looking for brevity."

Couple the practical need for succinctness with a desire to help her students see how ordinary events in every life are worthy of examination, and you get Ellis's passion for the radio story.

"Besides," she said, "creative nonfiction has really boomed in the last ten years. I want them to start seeing their own lives as really cool. And if you can write a good vignette, then you can write. That generalizes out into anything you're writing. So what I'm working on all semester is that kind of compressed experience . . ., how to get them to write a good nonfiction piece."

The inspiration for a radio show came to Ellis in one of those "aha" moments familiar to good teachers.

"I was riding on my bike," she said, "listening to *This American Life,* and I thought 'How can I get this element of storytelling into class?' That's when it hit me: *This Corvallis Life!* Besides, in creative writing, everybody tends to work on their own; there's no collaboration. So I thought, 'Here's a way to get students to work together. Here's a way to have a celebration in writing before they graduate.'"

The radio project has grown and matured over the four years Ellis has worked with it.

"At first I let them do the project as a performance piece," she explained, "but that didn't work out. They just got up and winged it. So that's when I said that they needed to create a permanent record, and that really raised the bar. The project evolved over the course of several years. It went from something they were winging to something that required fine-tuning, an audio or video piece, and it had to focus on life in Corvallis."

Ellis is particularly pleased with how the groups of three or four work together to combine individual voices within a single theme.

"For example, we had 'After Midnight' as a theme," she said. "Students explored life in our town after-hours. It seems like climbing to the top of the water tower and hanging out up there is something that's really popular. And you know, they talk about things that they really do; they don't hold back.... We have a grocery store in town, Cub Foods. It changed its name, but the kids still call it Cub Foods. One group did a really fascinating piece on the grocery store. They went around interviewing people who work there. . . . They've done radio shows on work and on play. One really moving piece was about this guy who had just taken driving lessons. He drove a girl to a top of a hill, and he talked about how he was nervous and that on top of the hill they were up in the sunlight, but they had to drive back down into the valley in the darkness. . . ."

Ellis said that definitive themes emerge from the radio stories the students produce.

"Lots of students have done stories about the train yard, which is a place they're not supposed to go.... That's a prominent theme," she said, laughing. "Places they're not supposed to go."

For the most part, Ellis' students create their audio theater projects using low-tech equipment: tape recorders.

"They write their stories, and they go into the other room with tape recorders," she explained. "They put up all these signs that say 'Quiet' and 'Keep Out.' Then they come back with their stories. I've found that the simpler they stay, the better they are. I had a group once that decided to burn their project onto a CD. The computer they had at home was far more advanced than our computer at school, so they ended up having to bring in all their computer stuff."

Ellis believes that the purpose for the student projects has little to do with the technology being used; rather, it has to do with creating a meaningful record of students' lives and experiences.

"I tell them, 'It has to be a permanent record,'" she said. "And I have to put a time limit on them. The whole thing should not be more than fifteen minutes long. Otherwise, they'll do these things that go on for half an hour. . . . Once I established the time limits, the projects became much livelier. Also, I said that each project had to have a narrator and music. And each person in the group needs to have their story included. Oh, and there can be *no* technical difficulties. If you have technical difficulties, I deduct points. That's why I really say 'Keep it simple.' Every semester I have someone say that they can do all sorts of cool stuff, but I know what happens: The computer dies. If it works, it's great. But when you're talking about a computer, that's a huge *if*."

Ellis never loses sight of *why* she wants her students to have the experience of producing audio theater.

"I want them to be better writers," she said. "Then there's the whole collaboration thing, which is essential. Plus there's the idea of really focusing on *listening* . . . and trying to bring a theme into everything. They have to work together; they have to decide on one person to speak for the group. I don't think they're learning a whole lot about technology, but they have to *listen* to a story. And they do enjoy it. Plus, this is a project that takes planning and coordination. All these kids are going to college, so they're learning how to plan their time so they're not scrambling the night before. My hope is that projects like this help them learn to manage their time. What I'm doing is setting them up to become more and more self-directed."

2

Constructing Knowledge with Video Projects

Much of today's technology helps students to construct their own knowledge—to learn by doing. The camcorder, for example, is an easy-to-use tool that can help students create a project in response to what they read in a fun, creative, and valuable way.

Consider this: a group of ninth-graders get together after school to tape an Oprah-style talk show featuring the characters from Orwell's *1984*. Students playing Julia, Winston, and O'Brien sit on a raised platform while the host—named Opera, to avoid any impropriety—points to a member of the "studio audience" who has her hand raised.

"This question is for Winston," the student in the audience says, hands on hips. "Why did you even *think* about Julia? Didn't you know it was a thought crime? Did you think you were so special that Big Brother wouldn't find out?"

Winston squirms in his chair. "I, uh…" he begins. But the irate questioner won't let him finish.

"You should *thank* O'Brien for helping you get your mind straight."

The audience erupts in applause, and Opera faces the camera.

"We'll hear from Winston and from the other members of the panel when we come back."

The camcorder pans to another area of the classroom where students have set up a parody of a paper-towel commercial.

And on it goes, for a full thirty minutes. The studio audience asks difficult questions, questions that usually start with the word *why*. The panel members answer in the voices of the characters they are portraying. Everyone has fun, and the taping results in a product everyone is proud of—a learning artifact, if you will. Once copies are made, each student gets to take the tape home to show his or her family, or to use as a study aid when final exams roll around.

Authentic Audience, Authentic Purpose, and Authentic Learning

On the surface, students think video projects are fun and certainly preferable to filling out worksheets. But the inherent value of this kind of activity is extensive.

Let's examine just some of the *learning* that takes place. First of all, students must work cooperatively to produce a video, and there is something for everyone to do. Those students who aren't thrilled about being in front of the camera can operate it, or write the script, or block the stage. They can help characters learn lines, or they can draw the posters that serve as backdrops. In essence, everyone is responsible for something, and the success of the project depends on each student doing his or her part. Learning to collaborate is one of the "soft skills" teachers are expected to encourage in the classroom, and video projects lend themselves to teamwork.

Second, students are working for a real purpose; they are *creating* something for an audience that goes beyond their teacher. Those who wouldn't study for a test if their lives depended on it learn all about key plot points and major themes of the story because they are actually involved in something bigger than themselves.

Most importantly, students are constructing their own understanding of the literature being studied—be it a novel, a poem, or a short story. In creating a video response, they process the main ideas of the literature by putting them into their own words. In essence, they internalize what the story is about. In the *1984* project, students drew conclusions about such themes as freedom of thought and freedom of speech, and they discussed at length the irony of a "talk show" about a book in which characters are not free to talk. In other words, they *experienced* the novel, and in doing so, they created their own understandings.

Constructivist theories suggest that children learn best when they devise their own knowledge by integrating something new with something that is already understood. In this case, students began with a format they knew well—the daytime talk show—and introduced something new: the characters and events from the novel. By assuming roles, students explored the real issues of the novel in a unique way. Furthermore, videotaping the activity provided an opportunity to involve those students who were reluctant to take part in the actual talk show, and it provided a tangible goal to work toward. In essence, technology can be the impetus for engaging students in the active construction of knowledge (Strommen 1992).

Because of today's testing hysteria, which is being imposed on our schools, some teachers might be hesitant to set aside the class time needed to create a video. But such hands-on projects may help students internalize the facts and events of literature better than typical worksheets and discussions. In my own experience, the students who created the *1984* video scored higher on the end-of-course test than those in the class that did not have access to the camcorder. Further, they had a more enjoyable experience with the literature. Of course, helping young people become lifelong readers is one of the most important goals of any English teacher.

Back when I did the *1984* project with my students, I knew little to nothing about how to guide students in the making of a video. My role consisted mainly of securing the camcorder from the library and saying "Good job" from time to time during rehearsals. I was pleased at how much students learned during the filming process, I enjoyed watching them work together, and the final product was good. I knew it could be better—there were several times in which the host had her back to the camera, for example—but I wasn't sure *how* to help my students make a more professional video.

I quickly learned that you don't have to be Quentin Tarantino to direct your students in a video project. You just need to know a few tricks of the trade.

Step 1: Selecting a Purpose and Roles

How students go about selecting the kind of video project they want to do is up to you. They can brainstorm ideas in small groups or discuss possibilities as a whole class. Simply acting out the best scenes from a book or short story is always a popular choice, as is adapting the story to a different format—*Romeo and Juliet* as an episode of *The Bernie Mac Show*, for example.

In brainstorming concepts for a video, students may propose ideas that are frivolous, too time consuming, or otherwise not tenable. Clearly outline expectations and explain that, as producer, you have the final say in "green lighting" a project.

However you choose to proceed, here are some guidelines to help the process go smoothly.

- **Select roles.**   A video project involves lots of work, so there is plenty for everyone to do. Some of the jobs that need to be filled for even the simplest of projects include director, assistant director, actors and understudies, scriptwriters, storyboard artists, equipment director, camera operators, cue-card technicians, light technicians, prop hands, and video editors. At first glance, you might think that the students writing and holding cue cards won't learn as much as the leading lady. But the cue-card techs have to write out each line of dialogue and pay close attention as it is being spoken. Similarly, the camera operator has to be exceptionally familiar with the script and with the overall vision of the project. In other words, *everyone* involved with the project is actively constructing his or her own understanding of the content. You will find a list of roles and their responsibilities at the end of the chapter.

- **Establish a timeline.** Clearly specify when each major section of the project is due. Set dates for the completion of the script and storyboard, for the memorization of lines, for filming, and for editing. A sample timeline is included at the end of the chapter.

- **Plan for pitfalls.** Allow some wiggle room in the schedule to deal with inevitable snags—the principal is certain to call a schoolwide assembly the day you're scheduled to begin shooting. Have your students brainstorm other possible snags so they can create contingency plans.

- **Encourage students to be creative.** Remind students that the goal of the project isn't to win an Academy Award. Let them use their imaginations to devise creative solutions to problems. For example, when my ninth-graders filmed a scene from *Fahrenheit 451*, they wrapped a stuffed toy in aluminum foil, and *voilà!* the Mechanical Dog.

Step 2: Storyboard and Script

When beginning a video project, it's often tempting to do what I did: hand students the camcorder and tell them to get to it. Believe me, that results in a lot of wasted time. Students may start filming before they even know what it is they really want to do. Consequently, it's not unusual for a project to go off on any number of unrelated tangents. Before you even check the equipment out from the media center, teach your students a few things about storyboarding.

Begin by explaining that a storyboard is a visual script. A storyboard clearly illustrates, scene by scene, what viewers will see and hear as they watch the video. The storyboard is similar to a comic strip; it is, therefore, the ideal way to involve those students who are constantly doodling in class. In fact, many comics have made the jump to the big screen easily. The Tom Hanks' movie *Road to Perdition*, for example, was originally a graphic novel.

A storyboard consists of the words, images, and sounds in each scene of the video. Essentially, it provides the *structure* of the project. Students can change their minds about the details of the storyboard once filming begins, but it serves as a model for the process—as well as another learning artifact. See Figure 2–1.

Each frame of the storyboard includes a sketch of what viewers will see; arrows indicate movement. Annotations alongside the sketches explain the scene ("Romeo gazes up at Juliet on the balcony."), and they outline what is heard ("Romeo exclaims 'It is my love!' as music rises.").

Some teachers have students write the script before turning it over to storyboard artists; others prefer that writers work in collaboration with artists so that there is a blending of word and image. However you choose to set up the process is, of course, up to you.

Step 3: Props, Costumes, Equipment, and Rehearsals

Depending on time, students can create elaborate settings and costumes, or they can make the best of the materials they have. For example, I know of a group of prop hands working on a *Romeo and Juliet* video who created masks for the ball out of construction paper and staples in five minutes flat. Another group shooting a creative response to *The Outsiders* let us know time had passed by filming a young man raising a large yellow paper circle—the sun—as another student read the line, "The next morning. . . ."

Rehearsals can also be a luxury of time. One of the nice things about video is that the camera operator can always reverse the tape if there is a mistake, or the editors can remove an error in editing. Actors can rely on cue cards, and the director can change a scene from day to night simply by turning out the lights.

As with costumes and props, equipment can be simple or complex. All you really need is a camcorder and a halogen lamp or other bright light source. You might also want to request a microphone or two, and don't forget a few blank tapes. If you have editing equipment or access to computer software such as Adobe Premiere or iMovie, so much the better. High-end equipment isn't critical to the project, however.

Step 4: Filming

The day of the shoot is usually hectic—and rewarding. Students run here and there, around the classroom, or the stage, or the cafeteria, or wherever you choose to film. Everyone has something to do, and they're doing it. Because this is a student-directed project, every person has a reason to participate. Again, this isn't just something the teacher told them to do.

The smoothness of filming is usually proportional to the amount of time invested up front, in planning. If the storyboards are detailed, and the cue cards are written, and the prop hands have brought in the boom box for the sound effects, then the director can shout "Action" with certainty that all will go as it should—unless there's a fire drill, that is.

Storyboarding a Video Project	Page __ of __

Title of project:

Brief description of storyline

Video (Describe in words what we will see on the screen.)	Diagram (Draw a simple sketch of what we will see.)	Audio (Describe in words what we will hear; include dialogue, sound effects, and music.)

Figure 2–1

Outside Projects: A Viable Option

With all the current emphasis on testing, many teachers are finding it harder and harder to do the sort of constructivist projects exemplified by videos. An option is to assign the projects to be completed outside of class, or to offer video projects as an alternative to an essay or paper. Of course, you won't be able to control the process as much with an outside project, but chances are you will still be very pleased with the result.

Assessment

Creative projects often resist cut-and-dried assessments. Even the best rubrics may pale in the light of authentic work. Before embarking on a video project, discuss with your students the best way to assess progress and performance. Involve them in creating meaningful and attainable goals for themselves, for their creative participation, and for the video itself.

The checklist in Figure 2–2 may provide a starting point from which to discuss assessment. Adapt it to meet your specific needs.

If we expect students to work together effectively, it may help to provide a rubric or checklist that outlines clearly the behaviors they should exhibit. Students who have not had much practice with cooperative learning may need to explore beforehand the *essence* of each element in the checklist below. In other words, you may wish to discuss with students specifically how each behavior may be manifested.

You can adapt this checklist to assess teamwork. For example, you may want to add a column in which students assess others in their groups. Access the companion website for printable checklists and links to rubric banks.

Video Projects in the Classroom: One Student's Perspective

When Bienvenido Concepcion was a junior at Glen Ridge High School in New Jersey, he read *Macbeth* like everybody else. But when it came time to complete a project, he did something just a little different: a video.

"The teacher, Mrs. Hearn, gave us a long list of things we could do for a project," Bien explains. "You could do a news article, an essay, an imitation book report. . . . One of the options was to reenact a scene from the story, so I asked if I could do a video, and my teacher said it was fine. That's when we decided to do the video."

The result, *Star Wars: Macbeth*, took Glen Ridge High School, and subsequently the Internet, by storm. You can watch the video by accessing the companion website for a link, or by searching for the key words *star wars macbeth*.

	Video Project Checklist	Points Possible	Points Earned: Self-Assessment	Points Earned: Teacher Assessment	Comments
1.	The video clearly reflects a major theme of the literature read in class.	10			
2.	The video is targeted toward a specific audience (children, adolescents, adults...).	10			
3.	The video has a clear purpose.	10			
4.	Each shot contributes to the video as a whole.	10			
5.	The shots flow together to create a unified product.	10			
6.	Music and sound effects are used effectively.	10			
7.	Lighting is effective; action can be seen clearly.	10			
8.	Actors or on-screen talent speak clearly and face the camera.	10			
9.	Props and costumes are used effectively; they do not distract from the overall product.	10			
10.	Language used is appropriate for the audience and purpose.	10			
		Total Points Possible: 100	Total Points:	Total Points:	

Figure 2–2

	Collaboration Checklist	Points Possible	Points Earned: Self-Assessment	Points Earned: Teacher Assessment	Comments
1.	Student actively helped the group achieve goals.	10			
2.	Student met individual responsibilities consistently and in a timely manner.	10			
3.	Student actively encouraged others in her or his group.	10			
4.	Student attempted to refocus group members who were off task.	10			
5.	Student praised his or her teammates often and sincerely.	10			
6.	Student phrased criticism in a kind and constructive manner.	10			
7.	Student freely contributed her or his talents and skills.	10			
8.	Student valued the talents and skills of all team members.	10			
9.	Student was flexible and adapted to specific situations.	10			
10.	Student maintained a positive attitude throughout the project.	10			
		Total Points Possible: 100	Total Points:	Total Points:	

© 2003 by Hilve Firek from *Ten Easy Ways to Use Technology in the English Classroom*. Portsmouth, NH: Heinemann.

Figure 2–3

Bien recently graduated with a degree in film studies from Penn State. He says that his path in film originated with the Macbeth video and with another video done for an English class: *Mission Impossible: Tom and Huck Rescue Jim.*

During the winter break of 1997, while most high-school students were sleeping or watching television, Bien and five friends filmed *Star Wars: Macbeth.*

"We got permission from the principal and the custodians to film inside the building under the condition that we wouldn't break anything with our fake lightsabers," Bien says. "My friend Michael McKoy wrote a script, which we adhered to rather effortlessly. The concept was simple . . ., there was a fight between good and evil—Macduff was good, Macbeth was evil. Macduff became Luke Skywalker, and Macbeth became Darth Vader. The dialogue would be an amalgamation of Shakespeare and Lucas. . . . Many sections were unchanged from the text, but others were changed to advance the plot and/or include a *Star Wars* reference. With a script, actors, a location, and a vague idea of what we were getting into, we set out to make the movie."

The action-packed video shows Darth Vader dueling it out in a lightsaber battle with Obi-Wan Kenobi, known to Shakespeare fans as Young Siward. The film also features a mad dash to the Millennium Falcon parked, thanks to the miracle of computer editing, in the school's gymnasium. The Luke Skywalker character of Macduff soliloquizes in the library, all the while hiding from enemy ships that can be seen through the windows.

Entertaining? Certainly. But did Bien and his friends *learn* anything?

"I can honestly say that when we acted the words out on the screen, I understood everything that happened. Believe it or not, doing that video got me into learning more Shakespeare. I read much more on my own. We learned *Romeo and*

Figure 2–4   A scene from *Star Wars Macbeth*

Figure 2–5 The magic of digital editing allowed the boys to "park" the spacecraft in their high-school gym.

Juliet in ninth grade, but I couldn't connect to the language until I analyzed it for the first time in preparing for the video.

"I mean, the video came out of nowhere. If you think about it, other people were turning in one-page projects. We spent a month on the video."

Equipment and Roles

All you really need for a video project are a few essential pieces of equipment:
- Camcorder and blank tapes
- Halogen lamp, or other bright light source

Other equipment can help make your video spectacular:
- Microphone
- Computer with editing software, such as Adobe Premiere
- Boom box, compact disc player, or other music source

Adapt this list of roles to meet the needs of your specific project:
- **Director** The director guides the actors in the performance of each scene. He or she also has the final word in the selection of music and props.
- **Assistant director** The assistant director serves as the liaison between the director and the other groups in the project. If the director is absent, the assistant director assumes all decision-making responsibilities.
- **Actors and understudies** Actors and understudies memorize the lines devised by the scriptwriters, and they learn the staging outlined in the storyboard. They listen to the director, and they incorporate suggestions

into their performances. In essence, actors breathe life into the project. *Note:* Understudies are *critical* for the major roles. Inevitably, the main character comes down with chicken pox on the first day of shooting.

- **Scriptwriters** Scriptwriters work with the storyboard artists to adapt a concept into words and images. Scriptwriters often modify the words of an original text to meet the specific needs of the project.
- **Storyboard artists** Storyboard artists sketch each scene of the video, from start to finish. They create the graphic illustration of the initial concept.
- **Equipment director** The equipment director is responsible for reserving and acquiring all equipment for the entire project. He or she examines the timeline to determine the specific equipment needs for each phase of the project.
- **Camera operators** The camera operators must have a strong understanding of the features of the cameras. They must also have thorough knowledge of the script and storyboard so that they know when to zoom or pan.
- **Cue-card technicians** Cue-card techs write essential dialogue onto large poster board. The cue-card techs follow the scene carefully, moving from one card to the next seamlessly. Each actor has her or his own cue-card tech.
- **Light technicians** The light technicians are responsible for adding or removing light to enhance the mood of a scene. Light techs should experiment with the best light for each situation. In essence, light should be bright enough that viewers can see an actor's features, but not so bright that it casts shadows.
- **Prop hands** Prop hands are responsible for creating or obtaining all the objects necessary for a scene. For example, if you were staging the brawl between the Montagues and Capulets, the prop hands would need to find or make swords.
- **Video editors** Video editors are adept at using your school's video editing software. They collaborate with the director to add titles, incorporate music, and blend one scene into another.

Sample Timeline

Adapt the timeline shown in Figure 2–6 to meet the needs of your students. Of course, no two projects will flow in exactly the same way.

Extending the Lesson

Digital camcorders, computer-editing software, and music can help any student video project appear professional. For example, middle-school students participat-

Day 1	**Brainstorm** Remind students that you, the teacher, are the producer and, as such, you decide whether to "green light" an idea. Students must "pitch" their ideas in a way that convinces you of their worth. Typical projects include reenacting scenes, restaging endings, and putting characters into different situations.
Day 2	**Review guidelines and criteria** Discuss the project's scope and decide upon assessment criteria. When first starting out, keep projects relatively simple. Distribute a list of roles and responsibilities and ask students to consider how they may best contribute.
Day 3	**Establish groups** Ask students to volunteer for roles, but remind them that the producer may reassign people and tasks. Have students break into groups and discuss their responsibilities.
Days 4–6	**Group work** Individuals in groups design and complete tasks. Actors discuss motivation and practice how best to convey emotions. Writers and storyboard artists develop the script and staging. Equipment directors arrange for cameras and lights, prop hands secure necessary objects, and so on.
Days 7–8	**Rehearsals** Have several run-throughs and work through bugs.
Day 9	**Lights, camera, action!** Shoot the project.
Days 10–11	**Computer editing** While editors put the finishing touches on the video, have students reflect on the experience in small group discussion and journal writing. Ask them to reflect on what they learned about the content and the process. Have them write suggestions for improving the project in the future.
Day 12	**Screening** Host a screening of the video for other English classes, for administrators, and parents.

Figure 2–6

ing in a summer GEAR-UP (Gaining Early Awareness and Readiness for Undergraduate Programs) camp at the University of Montana used digital camcorders and iMovie to create original videos and animation that they burned to CD.

Though the technology was cutting edge, the process for creating a digital video was the same as the one outlined in this chapter. Students collaborated on a concept, they wrote and sketched storyboards, and they shot and edited footage.

Nonetheless, technology is constantly changing, and you may choose to pursue the latest in digital video with your students. As video-editing software becomes increasingly affordable and easy to use, students may soon submit original DVDs as unremarkably as they turn in book reports.

With more advanced students, consider combining standards of learning in your video projects. For example, students in most grades are required to write persuasive essays. The video equivalent of a persuasive essay is the infomercial. What

Figure 2–7   Allen Bull Plume is filmed during one
of the University of Montana's summer GEAR-UP
camps by videographer Nathan Iron Heart.

might an infomercial for perfume look life if it featured Juliet? How about a commercial for combs and watches with the characters from "The Gift of the Magi"?

Similarly, music videos lend themselves to the richness of images found in poetry. Consider, for example, how a music video based on T. S. Eliot's "The Waste Land" might appear.

Typically, English teachers aren't exceedingly interested in the gadgets that accompany such projects. Rather, it is the expression of self through words and images that we find impressive. Technology can be the hook, but the construction of knowledge is what excites us.

Remember, the purpose of this project is not to turn out award-winning videos, though you may be pleasantly surprised at the products your students create. Rather, the purpose is to *engage* young people in the content of the English classroom, to involve them in the construction of knowledge, and to encourage them to find joy in reading and writing.

According to current U.S. Copyright Law, students may use images that they did not create in projects that meet educational objectives. To be covered, students *must* include the following statement at the beginning of any multimedia project that includes downloaded or recorded images, clips, or music: "Certain materials in this presentation are included under the fair use exemption of the U.S. Copyright Law and have been prepared with the multimedia fair use guidelines and are restricted from further use."

3

Television and Short Stories: Building a Bridge

With all the brouhaha surrounding personal computers, video games, personal digital assistants (PDAs), and the like, you might think that television has lost some of its power over the lives of young people.

Not so. The average American household has at least one television on for seven hours a day. According to a 2001 study, America's adolescents spend more time watching television than in any other activity—except sleeping. In other words, by the time they graduate, teenagers will spend about 12,000 hours engaged in formal classroom instruction and a whopping 15,000 hours in front of the tube.

As much as we'd like to think that all our children are rushing home to read a novel a night, we know that what many are really doing is watching hour after hour of television. And they're not watching C-SPAN or the Learning Channel. They're watching sitcoms, dramas, and made-for-TV movies.

Let's face it: television is king. It has a vicelike grip on young people. I remember vividly trying to excite a class of ninth-graders about a travelogue project.

"What would you like to see in your lifetime?" I asked the group of thirty or so dubious students. "The Taj Mahal? the Eiffel Tower? the Himalayas?"

A 14-year-old girl raised her hand. "Ms. Firek," she said, "you can see all that stuff on TV."

Critical Viewers, Critical Readers

Even if we admit that television has an almost hypnotic effect on children, why should we, as teachers of the English language arts, embrace it?

The answer is simple. Television can be a *bridge* between the culture of the home and the culture of the classroom. By capitalizing on the hold television has over kids, we can teach them to become critical viewers and, by extension, critical readers. We can teach them the relationship between what they see on TV and what they read in books. We can teach them how directors use dialogue, images, and sound to create an overall effect in much the same way that writers use words to create an overall effect. In essence, we can use television to *teach*.

Further, incorporating television into the classroom doesn't require adding yet another task to a schedule that's already bursting at the seams. Bringing in TV is simply a way of teaching the standard content of the English curriculum— reading, writing, speaking, listening, viewing, and responding—differently, in a way that might excite those learners who see little connection between what they learn in school and what they experience in their daily lives. We already help students see how authors use words to persuade, to inform, and to entertain. Exploring with students how these elements are used on television may lead students to have richer and more fulfilling encounters with written texts.

Television as Society's Storyteller

According to George Gerbner, a professor at the Annenberg School of Communication, "Those who tell stories hold the power in society" (1993). In humanity's past, parents, churches, politicians, and elders told stories. Today we get our stories, our mythologies, from television.

The teaching of language arts centers on the teaching of *story*. We teach children to read stories, to discuss them, to write them, and to listen to them. We teach them to understand how stories are crafted, how imagery and symbols are used, and how messages are conveyed. We teach them the elements of stories: character, plot, setting, conflict, resolution, denouement. We teach them to read between the lines, to find and express main idea and theme. We teach them to respond to what they read, to criticize and evaluate.

But in today's image-driven society, the teaching of critical reading can be difficult, at best. I know I'm not the only teacher who's been asked, "Why do we have to read the book when we can see the movie?"

English teachers can use television, as society's storyteller, to help students *understand* today's stories, today's mythologies. We can explore the human condition as it is revealed, accurately or not, on the small screen. We can teach students the process of viewing critically, and then lead them to the process of reading critically. Again, television can be the bridge between what students already do and what we want them to do in the language-arts classroom.

After all, constructivist theories suggest that students learn best when they create their own understandings, when they build upon what they already know. Whether they are aware of it or not, young people have a strong understanding of how television *works*. If they are watching sitcoms, they know that the problem-of-the-day will be resolved by show's end. If they are watching dramas, they know that some crisis will befall one of the main characters. By encouraging students to recognize this understanding, we can help them realize that what we're doing in the classroom isn't all that different from what they know how to do already.

Getting Started

The situation comedy is a good place to start in integrating television into the English classroom. Believe it or not, the sitcom is popular culture's version of the short story, replete with archetypes, recurring images, stock characters, and morals. Think about it: What was *Andy Griffith*'s Sheriff Andy if not the wise old man in young man guise? What was Mayberry if not Shangri-La, the land that time forgot? What was Aunt Bea if not the matron, the keeper of tradition and culture?

Indeed, the sitcom is America's version of the story, told not around the campfire, but around the glowing screen of the television set. In the story of the sitcom, we face fears, share hopes, and laugh at our own weaknesses exemplified in others.

Even a show as silly as *Gilligan's Island* can be viewed in terms of its greater story. The saga of seven mismatched castaways thrown together in difficult circumstances harkens back to the band of pilgrims in *The Canterbury Tales*. The seven must make do with each other and learn to get along, despite their disparate backgrounds. Their weekly adventures substitute for the pilgrims' tales.

You can even look at Gilligan and his compatriots as symbols of modern humanity. They are cast out of paradise, the "civilized world," into a land where they must fend for themselves. They adapt to their new surroundings while they wait to be rescued—for a savior, if you will. Granted, the example may be far-fetched, but it nonetheless illustrates the way in which age-old stories are refashioned for a modern television audience.

By asking students to identify elements of storytelling in sitcoms, you introduce them to the *process* of critical reading by applying it to a format they already know, a format that—for many students—may be less intimidating than fifteen pages of printed type. In teaching critical reading, we typically ask students to question, connect, predict, clarify, and evaluate. In teaching critical viewing, we ask students to do the same things, to practice the skills they need to read for understanding.

The Sitcom as Story

 To address the sitcom as story, ask your students to look for features common to both. Begin by reminding them of the elements of story:

- **Plot** For the most part, plot is built upon conflict: person versus person; person versus himself or herself; person versus nature. The struggles we face in life make up our stories; they reflect the good and bad of our existence. Conflicts escalate until they reach a turning point, a climax, and are resolved. In situation comedies, conflicts often center on a misunderstanding in a family or among friends. Because sitcoms are only thirty minutes long, the conflict and resolution are often easy to spot.
- **Character** We come to "know" characters from their speech, actions, physical descriptions, and the ways in which they interact with others. Both short stories and sitcoms have stock characters: people who exist mainly as a type, or even as an archetype.
- **Setting** The place of a story or television show lets us know what to expect. We know that a story set on a beach will differ substantially from one set in a hospital emergency room or on a starship. Sometimes the juxtaposition of setting with plot results in a deliberate attack on balance: Think of *Scrubs*—a comedy set amidst the life-and-death drama of a hospital. Because students can *see* the setting on a sitcom, they can easily identify it and relate it to the overall effect of the show.

Chances are, your students have identified these elements in short stories any number of times—on quizzes, on assignments, on multiple-choice standardized tests. But have they ever attempted to identify them in their favorite television shows? If not, they may be missing the connection between what they do every day and what they're asked to do in school. Students often complain that school has nothing to do with "real life," but each day they encounter stories presented on television. By helping them learn to "read" television, we reinforce the connection between the culture of the school and the culture of the home.

And unlike movies, which can take up almost three class periods, the thirty-minute television sitcom is easy to incorporate into the English class.

Critical Viewing Strategies

You can provide practice in critical viewing simply by bringing in a videotape of any popular TV show and guiding your students through the episode. To help your students learn to view critically, use the same active-reading strategies with which your students are already familiar. A critical viewing guide is included later in this chapter in Figure 3–1 and on the companion website.

- **Predict** Based on what students may already know about the program, ask them to predict what will happen. Stop the tape occasionally to ask them to describe what will happen next.
- **Connect** Ask students whether the characters on the show are like anyone they know in real life. Ask them to describe ways in which the characters are similar or different. Help them see that characters on television are often one-dimensional.
- **Clarify** Stop the tape regularly so students may summarize, in their own words, what they've seen.
- **Question** Guide students in questioning what they see. Ask them whether it's realistic for a problem to be resolved in thirty minutes or whether a character could behave in real life the way she or he did in the show. Ask them whether actions and consequences are realistically portrayed.
- **Evaluate** Ask students whether the episode was quality programming or whether it was merely entertainment. Ask them to explain whether they would watch the show again in reruns or if they change the channel.
- **Reflect** Ask students to write a journal entry reflecting on what they've seen. For example, if they were a character in the show, what would they have done differently? If they were in charge of the production of the episode, how would they change it?

Next, discuss how the elements of short story are used to relate events in a sitcom. Review plot, character, and setting, and discuss them in relation to the sitcom watched in class. Then ask them to brainstorm a list of current popular shows. Have them determine how many episodes contain variations of these stock characters:

- **Father knows best** Family comedies often center on a male authority figure who bumbles his way through daily activities, but whose hidden wisdom eventually saves the day. Actor Damon Wayons epitomizes this character on *My Wife and Kids*.

- **The do-it-all mom** Women's liberation notwithstanding, family situation comedies often feature a mother who bakes cookies, sews Halloween costumes, and has dinner on the table when the Father-Knows-Best character walks in the front door. She may have a job outside the home, but it is incidental to who she really is. The character of Peggy Hill on *King of the Hill* is a good example of the do-it-all mom.

- **The smart-aleck servant** From Florence on *The Jeffersons* to Niles on *The Nanny* to Geoffrey on *The Fresh Prince of Bel-Air*, the too-good-for-this-job servant serves as a foil to the upper-class doings of the main characters. The maid or butler or driver or babysitter provides a much-needed dose of common sense in nonsensical situations. Consider, for example, how Daphne's down-to-earth logic often bursts the inflated ego of Frasier Crane on the long-running series *Frasier*. Perhaps it is a reflection of today's economy, but the character of the smart-aleck servant isn't as prevalent as it once was.

- **The brainy kid** This is a child, boy or girl, too smart for his or her own good. The brainy kids excel in school, but they miss out on social interactions; their "book smarts" separate them from the "normal" world of childhood. Think of Malcolm from *Malcolm in the Middle* or Lisa Simpson from *The Simpsons*.

- **The cool kid** These are the characters that have it together. What they lack in smarts, they make up for in hip-ness. They represent what we all wish we could be: attractive, admired, young, and oh-so-cool. Though she's a bit older than most, Joan on *Girlfriends* is a good example of the cool kid.

- **The out-of-place best friend** The cool kid often has a best friend whose ineptitude serves to highlight the hip-ness of the main character. Nothing goes right for this character. He or she can't get a date, or can't keep a job. They struggle with their weight or with baldness or with bad breath. The comedy inherent in this character's failures gives us an avenue by which we laugh at our own shortcomings and our own fears about not succeeding in life. Fes, the exchange student on *That '70s Show*, is a good example, but George Costanza on *Seinfeld* is the quintessential out-of-place best friend.

Of course, you and your students will find many, many other stock characters in situation comedies, but this list is a good start. Challenge students to identify character types in sitcoms and explain their function in the story. For example, how do stock characters help us understand the plot or storyline? How do they help us understand the human condition and ourselves? Ask students to identify whether any of the short stories they've read in class contain similar characters.

Have them compare ways in which characters are developed in short stories to ways in which stock characters are used in television.

Conflict and Plot in Sitcoms

One of the things we like about situation comedies is the tidy resolution to conflict. Whatever problem the plot presents, it is usually resolved at the end of thirty minutes. If the brainy kid cheats on a test, rest assured that he or she learns that cheating isn't the answer to a tough situation. If the do-it-all mom burns the cookies, she learns that she is still loved by her family. If the cool kid wants a date with the new hottie on campus, he or she will be accepted or rejected within the thirty-minute time frame. By the last commercial break, warring factions will hug and make up, or they will be stuck together in an elevator until they learn to see things from the other's perspective.

Another key plot device in sitcoms harkens back to Shakespeare's day: the comedy of errors. Mistaken identities—and the situations that ensue—are good for laughs week in and week out. The evil twin or the nasty look-alike cousin is a staple on situation comedies. No worries, though. Everything will work out.

Sitcoms and Short Stories: Making the Connection

Are stock characters and expected plot devices as prevalent in short stories as in situation comedies? Or are characters in short stories more multidimensional?

Often we see glimpses of stock characters in notable short stories, but they are developed in ways not possible on a sitcom. For example, how is Waverly Place Jong in Amy Tan's "Rules of the Game" the Brainy Kid? In what way is her mother the do-it-all mom? How are they developed in more depth than the characters on television? Challenge your students to compare and contrast characters in short stories to characters in sitcoms. By leading them in the processes of critical viewing and critical reading, you can help them develop their own understandings of how messages are conveyed.

Your Homework Assignment: Watch TV

To help build a bridge between popular culture and the culture of the classroom, adapt the following activity to meet the needs of your students. Use their responses as the basis for a whole-class discussion, or for small-group work.

 Adapt this guide to meet the needs of your class. A printable form is available on the companion website.

Assignment: Critical Viewing of a Situation Comedy

Directions: Watch a thirty-minute sitcom that focuses on family life. Answer the following questions.

Before You View: Predict

1. What is the name of the show? How does the name cue me into what the show will be about?
2. What do I know about this show? What is it "about"?
3. From what I know about the show, I can expect to see the following:

While You View: Question, Connect, and Clarify

1. Who is the main character of the show? How do I know?
2. What is the main character like? Is he or she similar to any of the stock characters discussed in class? Is he or she similar to anybody I know in real life?
3. What are the supporting characters like? Are they similar to any of the stock characters discussed in class? Are they similar to anybody I know in real life?
4. What is the setting of the show? What is the time and place? Does a place like this really exist?
5. What is the conflict in the show? Is it person versus person? Person versus himself or herself? Person versus nature? Is the conflict realistic? Why/why not?
6. In what way is the conflict funny? What makes it funny? Is it the dialogue? The situation?
7. Do I know how the story will turn out? Why/why not?
8. What is the turning point in the conflict?
9. How is the conflict resolved? Is such a resolution realistic? Why/why not?

After You View: Evaluate and Reflect

1. In what ways was this show similar to other situation comedies I've seen? Does it remind me of other episodes of other shows?
2. In what way was the plot of this television show similar to—or different from—the plot of short stories I've read in class?
3. In what way were the characters of this television show similar to—or different from—the plot of short stories I've read in class?
4. How did the setting influence the plot?
5. If I were to change this sitcom to a drama, what would I need to change? What would I need to keep the same?
6. If I watch this show again next week, what would I expect to happen?
7. If I were to face a problem such as the one on the show, I would . . .
8. I enjoyed this episode because . . ., or I didn't enjoy this episode because . . .

Figure 3–1

TV in the Classroom: One Teacher's Experience

Ellen Krueger teaches English and mass media at Millburn High School, a school of 1000 or so students in central New Jersey. The coauthor of *Seeing and Believing: How to Teach Media Literacy in the English Classroom*, Krueger believes in the value of using television, even sitcoms, in school.

In a unit on the 1950s, Krueger uses shows like *The Adventures of Ozzie and Harriet* and *Dennis the Menace* to help her students examine the texts and subtexts of American life.

"I give students a handout for guided viewing on how American life is portrayed on TV," she explains. "I ask them to describe the characteristics of the sitcoms—how moms are portrayed, how kids are portrayed . . . and I ask them what the title reveals about the show. Look at *The Adventures of Ozzie and Harriet*. . . . There's nothing that they do that's very adventurous. From these shows we see how kids are portrayed as cute and dads know everything and moms vacuum with their high heels on. . . ."

Viewing television with a critical eye is just one of the many lessons Krueger hopes her students will internalize.

"I ask my students to describe the subtext of the show. Of course, the kids always want to talk about morals and family values. The shows from the fifties illustrate that even the best of families have their problems. Communication is an important subtext of these shows as is respect for your elders, sharing meals together, and the whole togetherness thing. And then I have them watch *Malcolm in the Middle*."

According to Krueger, asking students to compare and contrast shows from the Eisenhower era to shows on television today results in some serious thinking.

"It's amazing," she said. "I used an extraordinary episode of *Malcolm* that really did a good job of examining gender roles, of examining what is considered to be traditional and nontraditional. In this episode it's the mom who's the disciplinarian and the dad who is clueless. It was such a fun episode, and I know this sounds like a cliché, but learning and fun are not mutually exclusive."

Krueger uses these sitcoms as the basis for a number of writing assignments.

"I ask them to write about how are children are portrayed in the fifties and today. For example, how is Malcom like Beaver from *Leave it to Beaver*? I ask them to talk about the realism of *Malcolm*; you know, parents scream and kids talk back. . . . Writing about the media lends itself to all the modes."

One project Krueger finds particularly valuable is an outside viewing assignment.

"I ask them to do an outside viewing of a sitcom or drama . . ., to watch a show of their own choosing and to explain how the show is a representation of the American family, to explain how art imitates life. It's an active viewing experience.

"I tell them to plan their viewing ahead of time or tape the show. I encourage them to take notes as they view. They're required to write a two-sentence plot summary to prove they watched the episode. Other than that, I'm not really interested in plot. Next, the students have to come up with a thesis, something that addresses how the family was portrayed. Was the portrayal realistic, idyllic, exaggerated, traditional, nontraditional . . .? In the body of the paper, they discuss the representation using specific references to the show.

"There are so many things they can consider. For instance, are traditional gender roles assigned? What socioeconomic group is represented? Why is TV basically white, middle-class America? What is revealed about American culture in this episode? You can peel this down, one level after another."

To help her students become critical viewers, Krueger guides them in the process.

"I do a lot of active guided viewing," she explains, "and I always give prompts. Like reader response with literature, I do a lot of viewer response. They really start watching television differently."

It's more than an understatement to say that Krueger is enthused about using television in the classroom.

"I feel really gratified teaching media," she says. "I feel like I'm teaching them real-life issues. These shows are cultural artifacts. . . . It's who we are."

Extending the Lesson: Documentaries and Informational Texts

Increasingly, English teachers are expected to incorporate informational texts into the curriculum. After all, many of the passages on standardized tests are nonfiction. In reading these passages, students are often asked to identify the author's perspective and purpose, to distinguish fact from opinion, to recognize propaganda, and to make inferences.

To help students practice these skills and prepare for the reading of informational texts, consider integrating television documentaries into the English classroom. You can find quality documentaries on any number of channels—PBS, the History Channel, A&E, and the Learning Channel, to name just a few. If your school does not have cable, investigate Cable in the Classroom. It provides cable programming to schools at no charge.

Again, you aren't doing anything *additional* when you bring television documentaries into the classroom. Rather, you are teaching essential skills using a medium your students are already familiar with.

Guide your students in a critical viewing of a documentary. Stop the tape regularly to point out examples of cause-and-effect relationships, fact and opinion, and other key elements of nonfiction.

For example, in a recent Discovery Channel documentary on Gettysburg, one expert suggested that Pickett's Charge was doomed because of the presence of fences, something Pickett and his fellow generals had not taken into account. If you were using this documentary, you could stop the tape and address the issue of fact versus opinion. Is the expert's opinion valid? Why? What evidence does he cite? You could also talk about cause and effect. Did the presence of the fences *cause* greater Confederate casualties than anticipated?

Adapt the viewing guide in Figure 3–2 to meet your specific needs. A printable version is available on the companion website.

Extending the Lesson: Reality TV

So-called reality television is popular with today's young people. They tune in to daytime talk shows that feature every imaginable situation, to courtroom programming such as *Divorce Court*, and to prime time shows like *Survivor* and *Big Brother*.

Critics of reality TV say that viewers may develop skewed understandings of what constitutes real life. Viewers may not realize that the footage that appears to be "slice of life" is carefully edited for high drama and impact. In fact, directors of some daytime talk shows prep their participants, telling them exactly how to behave to cause the greatest reaction in the studio audience.

Such programs offer English teachers a way to help students recognize propaganda. Try watching a tape of a daytime talk show with your students, but be sure to preview it first. While watching, ask students to identify examples of stereotypes and loaded language, two commonly used techniques of propaganda. Be sure to point out exaggerated claims and half-truths that should not be taken seriously. Finally, talk about the ways in which the host stirs up the emotions of the audience.

After discussing the techniques of propaganda, distribute a pamphlet or brochure from any special-interest group. Ask students to identify loaded language, half-truths, and exaggerated claims. Have students explain how the writer attempts to stir up emotions in the reader, just as the host did on the talk show.

To help your students further understand propaganda, ask them to outline a reality show based on the information found in the brochure. For example, if you are using handouts from an environmental group, what might a day in the life of an environmental activist look like on television? Might the program include footage of protesters chaining themselves to trees? In other words, how might the information in the brochure be translated into "good television"?

Like it or not, the watching of television takes up much more of the "average" American's time than reading books. As language arts teachers we can help our students have a better understanding of what they watch. We can help them see that what we do in English classes is connected to the so-called "real world" in very tangible ways. And who knows? Maybe they'll even enjoy themselves.

Assignment: Critical Viewing of a Documentary

Before You View: Predict

1. What is the name of the show? How does the name cue me into what the show will be about?

2. What do I know about this show? What is it "about"?

3. From what I know about the show, I can expect to see the following:

While You View: Question, Connect, and Clarify

1. What is the main idea of this documentary? How do I know?

2. What details or key events support the main idea?

3. From what perspective is this story being told?

4. Is the documentary unbiased? Or does it have elements of propaganda? How do I know?

5. Does the documentary rely solely on facts? Or are opinions present?

6. Does the documentary include charts and graphs? If so, for what purposes are they used?

After You View: Evaluate and Reflect

1. The documentary was about…

2. The purpose of the documentary was to…

3. The intended audience was…

4. Did the documentary achieve its purpose? How do I know?

5. If I were the director of this documentary, I would have…

Figure 3–2

4

Movies and Novels: A Match Made in Hollywood

Why do we hafta read the book? Can't we just watch the movie?

I think most English teachers would agree that a movie is rarely an adequate substitute for a book. Together, however, they may provide a richer experience for your students than either would alone. Just as television provides a tool for teaching short stories, film offers a way to help you teach the concepts of the novel.

All of us best understand those ideas we can put into context. For example, if someone starts talking about the possibility of life on Pluto, our minds immediately access what we already know about a) the solar system, and b) life as we currently understand it. Similarly, if someone wants us to give us driving directions, he or she immediately starts by ascertaining information we have in common: "Do you know where the McDonalds on High Street is? No? How about the mall? Yes? Okay, as you head down High Street you'll pass the mall on your left. . . ."

Using film in our classrooms helps build a context for reading—and for writing, listening, speaking, and viewing. In essence, making use of a media students readily enjoy—movies—provides a means to really *engage* them in the skills of literacy and oracy. One way in which teachers use film to build a context for literature is by examining traits both have in common. Let's look at an example: A typical unit of literary study revolves around theme, say, the "hero in literature." Before you ask your students to analyze Odysseus, consider asking them to analyze Bruce Wayne in Tim Burton's *Batman* or Peter Parker in Sam Raimi's *Spider-Man.* (In fact, the recent spate of superhero films harks back to ancient tales of heroes with extraordinary cunning or power, such as Odysseus and Hercules.)

In essence, a careful look at the elements common to both novels and feature films can help you involve your students in the skills of analysis necessary for success in the English classroom—and in the world.

Elements of a Novel

Before you begin analyzing film with your students, consider reviewing the elements of a novel: plot, characterization, style, theme, setting, tone, and point of view. Your middle- and high-school students may be able to define these elements or identify them on a standardized test, but do they really understand them?

Helping your students internalize these elements will enable them to read more actively—and more critically—and discuss stories more articulately. One way to guide them to a greater understanding is to lead them on an examination of the same elements as they are seen in film.

Elements of film

Filmmakers use many of the same narrative tools that writers do, but they add visual and audio elements that contribute to meaning in unique ways. Let's look at the building blocks of film:

- **Plot** As with novels, plot is what the movie is about. It's the main story. As with books, plot is central to the quality of a film. No amount of special effects or film tricks can make up for an abysmal storyline. (Remember the 1998 version of *Godzilla?* The film's tagline was "Size Matters." One particularly harsh critic said that the director should have remembered "Plot Matters.")
- **Characterization** In film, characters are seen and heard as well as described. We understand them based on how we watch them behave and interact with other characters. In *Star Wars,* for example, we identify Han Solo as a rakish rogue based on his appearance, his dialogue, his action sequences, and the way he interacts with Princess Leia.
- **Style** Just as authors become known for a particular style, so too do filmmakers. Style is essentially *how* the story is presented on screen. David Lean, director of such great films as *The Bridge on the River Kwai, Lawrence*

of Arabia, and *Doctor Zhivago* is remembered for his epic style of filmmaking complete with weighty story lines, sweeping panoramas, huge casts, and rich cinematography.

- **Tone** Again, tone is associated with the feeling the work produces. For example, romantic comedies tend to be lighthearted whereas dramas tend to be more serious. Tone is communicated in film by a number of elements, including lighting, sound, and use of cuts. More about these in a bit.
- **Point of view** If we are meant to view a scene through a particular character's eyes, the director will use a point-of-view shot. For example, when we see the gigantic rock rolling toward us in *Raiders of the Lost Ark,* we are experiencing the scene from Indiana Jones' point of view.
- **Setting** Setting is the time, place, and circumstances of the film.
- **Theme** Theme is the message behind the plot. For instance, *Dr. Zhivago's* plot revolves around a young physician-poet in the Russia during the Bolshevik revolution. One theme is that artists *must* speak out, despite grave personal risks, in celebration of all that is beautiful and good amid all that is ugly and evil.
- **Motion and Special Effects** One reason we like film is because the moving pictures stimulate our imaginations. In our minds, we get to do things in the movies that we can't do in real life. We can ride along with the bad guy in a car chase or we can soar through outer space with the hero. Further, special effects communicate meaning. For example, we all understand that a young man and woman running through a meadow toward each other in slow motion is film-speak for romance. If you take the exact same scene and speed it up, the result is comedic parody.
- **Visual Imagery and Composition** Helping your students understand imagery that they can see may help them better understand the uses of imagery in writing. Filmmakers convey imagery by the way they set up shots, or single scenes, in a movie. For example, if a director uses a low-angle shot—the camera tilts up toward the scene—then he or she is letting us know that what we're looking at is important. After all, it looms above our perspective. Conversely, if a director uses a high-angle shot, we know that what we're looking at has been reduced in significance. How a shot is composed also conveys meaning. For example, where characters *are* in a shot—in relation to one another and in relation to objects—provides clues as to how we should interpret what we see. When we see Peter O'Toole, desert cloaks billowing in the wind, filling up the screen in *Lawrence of Arabia,* we know he is destined for greatness.
- **Lighting** Lighting is used to evoke an emotional response in the viewer. Well-lit scenes suggest openness, whereas darkly lit scenes make us think that someone is hiding something. Similarly, if a character is often shot in

shadows, we begin to distrust him or her. If light seems to radiate around a character, we know we've found our hero.

- **Sound** Sound and music convey meaning as well. Would *Psycho* be nearly as horrifying if it weren't for the screech-screech-screech we hear during the shower scene?

Filmmakers use a variety of other techniques to share their message, but the ones listed above are a good start. If you want to learn more about the vocabulary of film, access the companion website.

Making the Connection: Critical Reading and Critical Viewing

To help your students learn to "read" film, bring in a movie that relates to the theme of a novel you're reading in class. The film does not have to be the movie adaptation of the book. In fact, bringing in a film with a different plot helps students learn to recognize connections that aren't immediately obvious. For example, if you are reading *Old Man and the Sea*, bring in *Cast Away*. Ask your students to compare and contrast the fortitude of the main character in each work and to analyze the message that is being communicated about the human spirit. Or if you're reading *1984*, bring in *A.I.* Ask your students to identify aspects of today's society that could contribute to either interpretation of a possible future.

To help your students examine film critically—and to relate the process to examining a novel critically—ask them to complete the following guidesheet as they watch a film. A printable version of the form is available on the companion website.

Assessment Through Storyboards

To assess whether your students understand the connections between the elements of novels and the elements of film, ask them to select a scene from a novel they are reading in class and create a storyboard illustrating what it would look like—and sound like—on the movie screen.

Many DVDs include the original storyboards in their "special features." For example, the special-edition DVD of Tim Burton's *The Nightmare Before Christmas* contains a storyboard-to-animation sequence that presents the storyboard at the bottom of the screen while the finished scene runs at the top. Consider showing one of the features to your students to help them understand the role of storyboarding in actual filmmaking.

Adapt the storyboard form below to guide your students' work. You can access the printable form on the companion website.

Critical Viewing and Critical Reading Guidesheet		
	Title of Movie:	Title of Novel:
Plot:		
Characterization:		
Style:		
Tone:		
Setting:		
Theme:		
Point of view:		
Motion and special effects:		
Visual Imagery and composition:		
Lighting:		
Sound:		
Your overall impression:		
© 2003 by Hilve Firek from *Ten Easy Ways to Use Technology in the English Classroom*. Portsmouth, NH: Heinemann.		

Figure 4–1

Storyboarding a Scene from a Novel	Page __ of __

Title of novel:
Brief description of scene to be storyboarded:

Page numbers in book:

Video (Describe in words what we will see on the screen.)	Diagram (Draw a simple sketch of what we will see.)	Audio (Describe in words what we will hear; include dialogue, sound effects, and music.)

Figure 4–2

Extending the Lesson: Graphic Novels and the Silver Screen

Many of today's directors turn to graphic novels and comic books to find their inspiration for film. As I noted in Chapter 2, the movie *Road to Perdition,* directed by Sam Mendes and starring Tom Hanks, was based on the graphic novel of the same name. Similarly, the film *Ghost World* starring Thora Birch was based on the sequential-art book written by Daniel Clowes.

Directors appreciate graphic novels because they are laid out in much the same way as storyboards. In other words, the illustrations in the comic panels help a filmmaker to picture in his or her mind exactly *how* the story might translate to the screen.

As an option to storyboarding, ask students to select a scene from a novel and convert it to comic book form. Use the comics to assess student understanding of plot, characterization, setting, and tone. For more on using comics in the English classroom, access the companion website.

Movies: The Main Course, Not Dessert

Mary T. Christel is a coauthor of *Seeing and Believing: How to Teach Media Literacy in the English Classroom.* She's also a communication arts teacher at Adlai E. Stevenson High School in Lincolnshire, Illinois, a suburb of Chicago.

She knows firsthand the power of film in the English curriculum.

"Well," Christel began, "if we're looking to make reading relevant to kids, there are many ways to pair classic texts with popular-culture adaptations of those texts. You can use companion films or you find movies that address similar themes but which come from a different culture.

"For example, I taught Ibsen's *A Doll's House,* and I would pair it with an Australian film called *My Brilliant Career* because it dealt with a strong-willed woman at the turn of the century who didn't see marriage as a necessary option for her. The students could see the connections to *A Doll's House....* They could see the pressures that were put on her. There's a South American film I pair with *A Doll's House* as well; it's called *The Official Story.*"

Christel recognizes that many English teachers look immediately for a book's companion film, but she often prefers to bring in a movie that represents a different culture but which has a similar theme.

"For example," she said, "when I teach *All Quiet on the Western Front,* I use an Australian film, *Gallipoli.* Again, it deals with a lot of the same themes: relationship issues, the hardships of wars. . . . It looks at World War I from many levels."

Christel believes that bringing film into her English class exposes young people to a variety of artistic interpretations.

"These films open kids up to a broader range of stories and ideas and context," she explained. "Not that teaching literary adaptation films is necessarily bad. It's more natural, but it can reinforce the idea that it's more painless to watch the movie than to read the book."

Critical to integrating film into the curriculum, Christel believes, is moving beyond narrative structure.

"I really want kids to engage in a critical analysis of film," she said. "I want them to go beyond the narrative. I teach a film analysis course, and I try to bring some of the skills I teach in there into my English classes. For example, I try to get kids to recognize some of the choices directors must make—composition, music, casting, sound effects—and to address what a film can do that a written piece of literature cannot. Not that one is better than another, necessarily, but that film has a language of its own, an expanded vocabulary."

While Christel sometimes has her students shoot their own video, she generally prefers to keep her English classes "low-tech."

"I do more production work in my film analysis class," she said, "but there are bunches and bunches of activities you can have kids do. Something I do is try to keep it low-tech; otherwise it can become too cumbersome."

Storyboarding is a simple activity that can help students begin to think like directors.

"What I'll do is get the students to select an important moment from a novel and create a storyboard," she said. "They can plan the kind of sound, dialogue, music, sound effects, or voice narration that they would include. That really gets the kids into thinking like a director."

If Christel had to select just one piece of advice for English teachers who want to integrate film into their classrooms, it would be this: engage students in critical viewing.

"Teachers need to set a purpose for viewing," she explained, "and they need to get the kids to do something while they're watching film. I get frustrated when people use film for babysitting or for dessert. They show the film and then say, 'Okay, kids, what'd you think?' They don't treat film as a legitimate and rich text; it's just something to fill time. It's hard to get them to see that they should get kids actively involved in the viewing. But you would never give a kid a book and say read it and then just say 'What'd you think?'"

Just knowing some of the language of film can help English teachers guide their students in a critical analysis, Christel believes.

"There has to be some kind of systemized instruction attached," she said. "There needs to be a purpose and a system of *how* you want the kids to investigate a film. And you have to hold kids accountable for doing it. For example, if they've missed part of the film, they need to make arrangements to make it up. You wouldn't let them just 'miss' the middle of a book, would you?"

Sometimes kids are initially reluctant to put their brains to work while watching a movie, Christel said. But she added that eventually they appreciate being able to discuss something that is such a large part of their lives with more conviction.

"Sometimes they feel like I'm going to spoil their fun," she explained. "But they are pretty savvy when it comes to media, and they really appreciate getting a vocabulary so they can talk with clarity about something they enjoy."

Christel says that English teachers who wish to learn more about media literacy need only log on to the Internet or visit their local bookstore.

"Teachers shouldn't be afraid to try new things," she said. "There's so much material out there to help them acquire the language to talk about film. We *do* need to use media in a thoughtful way. The kids are consuming so much of it, and they're doing so indiscriminately."

5

Keypals: Toward a Global Understanding

English teachers have long relied on pen pal projects to engage students in writing for real purposes and real audiences, but computer technology has made communicating with others around the world easier than ever.

Keypals, or electronic pen pals, help students learn to view themselves in relation to the world at large. As students share experiences with one another, global understanding is increased—and communication skills improve. Further, students develop respect for diversity, both in language and opinion. Reading and writing are valued because students come to see them for what they are: real tools for communication.

But email is not without inherent problems. If you have a free Web-based email account, chances are you've received more than your share of spam, or junk email. And quite a bit of spam is obscene . . . to put it mildly.

English teachers who want to use email to help them meet educational objectives do have options. A number of places on the Web offer free, safe email for kids, and there are numerous sites that connect classrooms with one another. But first, let's examine the benefits of keypals in the English classroom.

Keypals: What's the Point?

Those of us who work with reluctant learners tend to do everything we can, short of actual cartwheels, to help students discover the joy of reading and writing. We invite authors to visit our classrooms, we invite peer collaboration, and we read and write *with* our students. We also try to engage students in the writing process by asking them to write for real purposes and real audiences. Enter the traditional pen pal project.

One summer, I taught exposition to seniors who had failed the course previously. To say these students were reluctant readers and writers is an understatement. After all, they had been denied graduation the previous June, and here they were in summer school. They were *not* happy.

I tried everything I could think of to get them involved. I brought in movies for them to respond to. I invited guest speakers to talk about writing. I took them outside for inspiration. In fairness, the students did what they were assigned—they weren't going to fail again—but they were bored and disinterested. That's when I had the bright idea of pen pals.

At the time, I was participating in a listserv, an email discussion group, for English teachers. I posted a request for pen pals and quickly connected with a teacher in northern Virginia. She was excited about the idea, and soon I had an envelope in my hand with letters from her summer-school students to mine. I distributed the letters and asked my students to respond. I was pleasantly surprised when they began talking animatedly with one another and passing around the class photograph included with the letters.

The next thing I knew, pens were out and letters were being written. I was so very proud . . . and of course we all know pride comes before a fall. Needless to say, I was heading for one heck of a stumble.

That night I eagerly read what my students had written to their peers. As I read, I came to the realization that I couldn't mail the letters. They had written about their lives, but sadly, their lives were filled with the grit of the inner city. Their letters included invitations to visit and "hang out," genuine heartfelt sentiments from one group of teens to another, but the descriptions of what they would do together would have landed me in jail for contributing to the delinquency of minors had I mailed the letters to their suburban counterparts.

I had made a serious error. I had failed to give any real directions. I had failed to *structure* the project. In my youth, all I had said was, "Write."

I learned a great deal from that blunder. One: I learned that kids *will* write, and they will write descriptively, from the heart, if they are given a real reason to. Two: I learned that projects must have structure. In my zeal for authentic learning, I neglected to design the project for success. Consequently, it failed. Three: I learned that kids must be protected from themselves and others. What if I had mailed the letters, and the two groups had gotten together and embarked on something illegal? I learned that my moral obligation to my students—and to their peers—extended beyond my classroom walls. If I were going to open my classroom to the world, I had better be prepared to help my students navigate their way through it safely.

Keypals: A Faster, and Perhaps Safer, Alternative

In essence, writing for real reasons and for real people helps students discover the joy of authentic communication. Keypal projects add immediacy to the excitement of real writing, and we all know that immediacy is critical when working with kids. With keypals, students no longer have to wait weeks for letters to arrive from far-off destinations. The quick turnaround time may even help contribute to *better* written communication, though email writing may initially appear careless:

> Technically, the writing in an email message may be sloppier and more ambiguous, but it permits a genuine ease of communication, especially for students who do not like to write. As they get involved in an email correspondence, however, they might become aware of the possibilities for communication and miscommunication in new ways. If a sentence in a message they receive is not clear, they can shoot back a question. If they gather from a response that they have not made themselves clear in a message, they can shoot off a correction or an addition. Exchanging email can thus become a process of revision. (Brunner and Tally 1999, 149)

In other words, writing for real communication *teaches* students the reason we write: to be understood. Moreover, the quickness with which email is sent lends itself to immediate feedback: either the message is clear or it isn't. Perhaps best of all, students learn to self-correct.

 Because email can be spammed, many sites build in safeguards for email exchanges. One of the most popular—and safest—sites on the Web for finding keypals for educational purposes is ePALS.com.

To date, more than four million users have signed on to take advantage of ePALS's free services. To ease fears, ePALS features monitored email and profanity filters.

Teachers can register with ePALS for free, and they can search for partner classrooms in countries all over the world. They can also browse project ideas and participate in teacher-to-teacher discussions. Further, each discussion area includes a translation option, so if someone sends you an email in French, you can translate it in one click.

Of course, students can also register for their own free ePALS accounts. They can then search for individuals to correspond with, or they can participate in group projects and book discussions.

A much smaller site is the Intercultural Email Classroom Connections page at www.iecc.org. Teachers and students can elect to participate in listservs or in online forums. Similarly, kidlink.org connects individual teens to one another, and a special section for teachers offers language-arts lesson ideas. *Remember:* All Web addresses are subject to change, so check this book's companion website for the latest links.

A word of caution: If you look for keypals in a standard search engine such as Google, or in a directory like Yahoo, you'll find lots of sites, but many are inappropriate for children.

The ePALS site offers free, filtered email accounts for kids. So, too, does Gaggle.net, though its free service is dependent on advertising. A number of subscription email filtering services have hit the market lately; one of the best is Bsafe (www.bsafehome.com). At present, it costs about $40 per year.

Structuring Your Keypal Project for Success

The structure of your keypal project will probably be similar to other project-based learning activities you've been successful with. Begin by discussing learning objectives with your students. What is it you want them to achieve? For example, do you want them to analyze a current event from another's perspective? Do you want them to share ideas about a novel they're reading in class? Do you want them to practice writing for effective communication? In essence, identify, up front, the learning you hope the keypal project will enhance.

Next, identify the project specifics: How many keypals should students seek out? How many email should they expect to exchange, and how often? Will they have time to email their pals in class? You might also want to outline in advance a timeline for the project.

Ask students to archive all the messages they send and receive. Also, advise them that all messages are subject to being read by anyone in class at any time. Remind them that this is a class project, and, as such, the writing is *always* subject to peer and teacher review.

Once you've decided on the nuts and bolts of the project, review basic netiquette and Internet safety with your students.

Netiquette: The Niceties of Email Messaging

Netiquette, or email etiquette, is the basic rules for communicating electronically. Because tone may be difficult to "read" in an email, appropriate netiquette may help stave off a barrage of angry messages or flames. (A drawn-out exchange of angry emails is known as a flame war.) It is considered bad netiquette, for example, to type email messages in all caps. A message written in capital letters is considered to be the same as shouting. Further, it is a good idea for students to avoid using sarcasm in messages, especially if they are communicating with keypals for whom English is not the first language. Sarcasm is often difficult to interpret without vocal inflections. The same goes for humor. If your students must make a joke, ask them to indicate that they're kidding with an appropriate emoticon. Emoticons are icons that denote emotions. For example, to indicate a joke, type a semicolon, a dash, and the closing parenthesis. If you tilt your head, the result looks vaguely like someone winking:

;-)

To find other emoticons, simply type the word into any search engine or go to this book's companion website.

Talk with your students about whether they should include Netspeak in their messages. Netspeak is made up of acronyms that the English-speaking Internet community has, by default, agreed upon. One of the most common examples of Netspeak is BTW, short for "by the way." Others include IMHO (in my humble opinion), IMNSHO (in my not so humble opinion), AFAIC (as far as I'm concerned), LOL (laughing out loud), ROTL (rolling on the floor laughing), and many more. To access a dictionary of Internet acronyms, connect to the companion website.

Finally, remind students that offensive, vulgar, or inappropriate language is unacceptable.

Internet Safety: Just Be Smart

It seems like every time you turn on the news, you hear a story about a kid being abducted by someone he or she "met" on the Internet. But when you consider how many people are on the Net, the chances of being victimized are really quite small. Nonetheless, establishing some basic guidelines will help to ensure a safe and enjoyable keypal experience for all.

First and foremost, remind your students to never, ever give out personal information to anyone they meet on the Net, no matter how "nice" the person seems to be. That means no exchanging phone numbers or snail-mail addresses. Period.

Similarly, remind students to never, ever agree to meet a Net acquaintance in person. That means no meeting at the mall or at the local bowling alley. That means no meeting anyone, anywhere, at any time. Period.

Analyzing Critical Thinking: One Way to Assess Keypal Projects

How you assess student learning in a keypal project depends on the objectives you want learners to achieve. A popular way to evaluate student participation in keypal projects is to analyze the thinking demonstrated in the written messages.

Are you thinking critically? Do you . . .	
3	• Interpret written messages accurately? • Ask for clarification when necessary? • Reply appropriately? • Attempt to understand your keypal's perspective? • Explain your perspective rationally? • Try to be fair?
2	• Misinterpret messages regularly? • Fail to ask for clarification? • Ignore your keypal's point of view? • Seldom explain your perspective? • Base your decisions on poorly conceived notions?
1	• Dismiss your keypal's perspective, opinion, or point of view as irrelevant? • Ignore facts because they counter preconceived notions? • Demonstrate close-mindedness? • Demonstrate prejudice or bias? • Respond to email messages in a hostile or arrogant manner?

Figure 5–1

 Consider assessing students' critical thinking skills by adapting the rubric shown in figure 5–1. Access the printable chart on the companion website.

Building the Global Classroom

Dwayne Voegeli, a teacher at Winona Senior High School in Winona, Minnesota, wanted to help his students understand that the world is actually a very small place.

"I was looking for a website that could help me better connect students in my classroom with students around the world," Voegeli explained. He stumbled upon ePALS, a site that connects classrooms via a very easy to use technology: email.

"I know most people think all kids are real techno-wizards, but for most of my students, that's not true," he said. "So we started with a really basic assignment: Each student was to meet one new friend from somewhere around the world, and they had a whole quarter to do it in. I pointed them to the ePALS site, and they each got an account there. Then they went looking for friends."

What began as a simple email assignment grew into collegial relationships between Voegeli's students and students in Sweden, Germany, and Japan. Two summers ago, Voegeli even took his class on a trip to Europe to meet some of their ePALS, and several teachers from overseas have brought their students to visit his school in Minnesota.

"I think it's really important for kids to talk with their peers around the world," he said. "They begin to look at current events from many perspectives, and they share their ideas in their own words, in the language that kids use. They process the information we learn in class better because they have an emotional connection. . . . They're involved."

That emotional connection contributes to better learning experiences, Voegeli asserted.

"Textbooks are a good source of information," he said. "But projects where kids communicate with each other . . ., those are much more engaging. They target that affective domain; they engage the kids on an emotional level and grab their interest. I truly believe they learn more things—and better—with a person-to-person connection."

Voegeli said that having keypals has excited some students beyond his initial hopes.

"Some of the kids who have Net access at home, they can't get enough of it," he said. "If they're home, they're logged on, talking with their friends in other countries."

Like many teachers, Voegeli has to take his students to the computer lab so that each of them can access the Internet.

"Obviously, that's a huge limitation," he said. "But it's worth the effort to get them there."

Voegeli's students completed a joint survey on the recent crisis in Iraq with students in Sweden, a project that required students to carry out thorough research, conduct effective interviews, and process their findings in writing for publication on the Web. If you'd like to learn more, a comprehensive description of this project is on the companion website.

"We started by doing some background research on our end," he said. "We did some pretty in-depth study. Then each student had to interview four or five other students—for a total of about 130 students—and compile the results and do the percentages. The kids in the Swedish classroom also did background research, and they interviewed a total of 89 students." The chart shows their results.

Voegeli "met" his colleague in Sweden through the Internet, and the two have been working collaboratively, mostly through email, for the past three or four years.

"We've done a lot of projects, but this is the first time we've done a survey," Voegeli said. "It was very, very successful. It's such a good way to get kids involved in the content and involved in what's going on in their world."

Iraq crisis survey results		
Questions:	**Winona Senior High School, Winona, USA**	**Fredrika Bremergymnasiet, Haninge, Sweden**
1. Do you support the U.S. Government attacking Iraq if the United Nations approves of the action?	Yes: 48% No: 32% No Opinion: 21%	Yes: 37% No: 47% No opinion: 16%
2. Do you support the U.S. Government attacking Iraq if the United Nations does NOT approve of the action?	Yes: 19% No: 57% No Opinion: 24%	Yes: 14% No: 74% No opinion: 12%
3. Do you see any advantages to the war?	Yes: 36% No: 49% No Opinion: 16%	Yes: 35% No: 48% No opinion: 17%
4. In what way do you think an attack against Iraq would affect you?	Positive: 18% Negative: 53% No Opinion: 29%	Positive: 11% Negative: 46% No opinion: 43%
5. Thinking of the way President Bush has pursued the matter, do you think Al Gore would have acted differently?	Yes: 56% No: 13% No Opinion: 31%	Yes: 36% No: 25% No opinion: 38%
6. How do you think the U.S. economy would be affected by a war?	Positive: 21% Negative: 64% No Opinion: 16%	Positive: 16% Negative: 63% No opinion: 21%
7. Why do you think President Bush wants to attack Iraq? You may circle more than one choice:	Stop terrorism: 30% Help the people of Iraq: 6% Global Security: 16% Oil: 18% Power and Control: 27% Other Reason(s): 2%	Stop terrorism: 10% Help the people of Iraq: 4% Global Security: 12% Oil: 33% Power and Control: 23% Other Reason(s): 18% (finish Bush Sr's work, revenge)
8. Do you think that the proof of Iraqi weapons of mass destruction is enough to justify an attack on Iraq?	Yes: 44% No: 35% No Opinion: 21%	Yes: 36% No: 54% No opinion: 10%
9. What opinion do you think the Europeans have towards the war?	In favor of a war: 14% Against a war: 57% No Opinion: 35%	In favor of a war: 9% Against a war: 73% No Opinion: 18%
10. President Bush has described the war as a case of good vs. evil. Do you think that is the case?	Yes: 40% No: 46% No Opinion: 14%	Did not respond
11. Do you think you would support the U.S. government attacking your country?	Yes: 7% No: 80% No Opinion: 13%	Yes: 6% No: 86% No Opinion: 8%

Figure 5–2

6

Interactive Writing: The Simple Wonders of Word Processing

I asked a local high-school principal what he remembered most about his former English classes.

"Ugh," he replied, with a shudder. "My English teacher made my life miserable."

For some reason, I take everyone's experiences with language arts personally, and the principal's remark wounded me.

"But why?" I asked.

"I wrote essay after essay, and nothing I wrote was ever any good," he explained. "My teacher had that famous red pen. I dreaded getting papers back because she really tore them up."

"Why were you writing?" I asked.

"What?" He looked puzzled, so I tried rephrasing the question.

"What was the reason you were writing?"

The principal looked at me as if I'd lost my mind.

"We were writing because she said to."

Interactive Writing for Real Audiences

Quite often, we English teachers ask students to write as a form of scholarly exercise. We teach exposition, so we tell students to expound. We teach persuasive writing, so we require the writing—and rewriting—of persuasive essays. But we tend to teach writing in academic isolation. Students learn quickly that composition is a task to be done in language-arts classes for English teachers. For example, if the science teacher asks students to keep a journal, chances are pretty good that students will protest . . . loudly.

"This isn't English class. Why do we have to write in here?"

The compartmentalized and departmentalized nature of schools is partly to blame. Because we are under so much pressure to meet the narrowly delineated standards in our subject areas, we rarely get a chance to address the transference of knowledge to fields other than our own. Luckily, technology may provide a way to help us show students that writing is not just some form of punishment doled out by sadistic English teachers; it a *real* pursuit that must keep a *real* audience in mind.

Interactivity is a term much bandied about by computer geeks. Though it may imply different things to different people, most agree that *interactivity* suggests an action on the part of a *user*. In other words, the reader or the participant will be expected to *do* something, such as click an icon or make a decision. Therefore, developing a thorough understanding of *audience* becomes critical for writers who wish to add interactivity to their work.

In essence, the promise of interactive writing is that it may help students better comprehend *audience*. If a writer is not aware of what a reader *needs*—the reader's *purpose* for reading—then he or she will have no idea what to include.

I remember struggling with one particular ninth-grader about audience. I asked him to read another student's paper as an example. I then asked, naively to be sure, "Do you see the difference?"

"Yes," he replied. "That paper is longer."

Adding interactivity to a word-processed document *requires* that the writer consider the point of view of the reader—to fully understand his or her audience. Consider, for example, an interactive version of *Little Red Riding Hood.* Written for an audience of elementary-school students, the story might look something like Figure 6–1, which shows just the top of the document. If you access the entire interactive story on the companion website, you will find that the story continues as the writer offers any number of options for the reader. It's not hard to see why many students who don't like traditional writing find interactivity appealing. There's a certain mystery to it. Furthermore, writers of interactive stories must put themselves in the minds of their potential readers. They must ask themselves, "If *I* were reading this story, what would *I* think? What choices might *I* make?"

The Adventures of Little Red Riding Hood

  ←——— Double-click on the speaker icon to hear a wolf howl!

Wasn't that **SCARY**?

Now imagine that you're a little girl, only five or six years old.
You have to walk through the deep, dark woods to take dinner
to your grandmother. Off in the distance, you hear that sound.
What do you do?

Click <u>here</u> to run home and hide under your bed.

Click <u>here</u> to continue on through the deep, dark woods.

Click <u>here</u> to learn more about wolves from the National Geographic website.

Sound clip and photograph downloaded from <u>dgl.Microsoft.com</u>.

Figure 6–1

Students who develop a comprehensive understanding of audience become mature writers. They have no problem switching between the cyber-slang of Net messaging and the college application essay. They consider what their readers *need,* and they write accordingly.

Word-processing packages, such as MS Word, offer options that make it fairly easy for writers to add interactivity—and other features to engage a reader, like sound—to their writing. For example, to move readers from one part of a document to another, students can insert "bookmarks," codes in the document, and then add hyperlinks to each bookmark. These features enable readers to follow their own interests in a story, to decide where to go next. For example, in the *Little Red Riding Hood* story, the writer inserted bookmarks that took readers to different locations, depending on how they answered a specific question. Even pictures and clip art can be made into links. (Because word-processing software varies, check the Help file to learn the specifics of adding interactivity for your specific program.) Again, for bookmarks and hyperlinks to be effective, writers must have a thorough understanding of audience. They must anticipate what will engage their readers—and they must also anticipate what may distract them. Too many options and too many links can be overwhelming. Adding interactivity requires that students learn the meaning of constraint.

Writers can also insert hyperlinks to the Internet in their word-processed documents. I know some teachers who require hyperlinks in word-processed research papers whenever a reference to the Web is made. They can then connect directly to the site to determine whether information has been plagiarized.

You may find that adding a hyperlink is surprisingly easy. In Word, for example, simply select the text you wish to link and click Insert on the Menu Bar at the top of the screen. Bring your cursor down to Hyperlink and click. A dialogue box will appear; type in the Web address you wish to link to. (Be sure to type in the entire address, including the "http://" part.)

For example, if you wanted to link a vocabulary word to an online dictionary, you would drag your cursor over the word to select it and click Insert > Hyperlink. You would then type in the dialog box *http://www.dictionary.com*.

Now when you read your Word document on the computer, the word is underlined, indicating that it is hyperlinked. Click on the word, and *voilà!* Dictionary.com will open in a new window.

Interactivity and Visual Literacy: Understanding the Message Through its Media

By incorporating interactivity and other options, students can vary the way text *looks* to convey meaning. For example, in Figure 6–1, the word *scary* is in a spooky-looking font. Granted, this feature isn't exactly glamorous, but visual learners may begin to associate the way text looks with its message. For example, examining design and layout can be a good prereading step for reluctant readers; they may be able to ascertain tone and audience before reading a single word.

Notice also that the interactive version of *Little Red Riding Hood* is laid out differently than a traditional word-processed document might be. Because writers design interactive stories to be read on a computer screen—not on paper—words are arranged in boxes, known as text boxes. Writers must determine where these boxes go so that readers may understand; again, the crucial concept of audience is reinforced. Text boxes can also be formatted to add color, shadows, and other visually pleasing effects. Furthermore, students can add clip art, illustrations, and pictures that contribute to the totality of the message. In essence, the ways in which words are displayed become as much a part of the overall message as the words themselves. If a student learns to use bookmarks, hyperlinks, text boxes, color, fonts, and other word-processing features effectively, he or she learns to accommodate the needs of the reader. And isn't that what all "real" writers hope to do?

Getting Started

Step 1: Begin with Something Familiar

One problem with interactive writing is that students—and teachers—can get confused in the storyline. To help alleviate this, have students begin with fiction stories everyone is familiar with—fairy tales, for instance. Once students become proficient with the nuts and bolts of adding interactivity, they can move on to other genres and other writing modes; the positive reasons for using interactivity—demonstrating an understanding of audience, integrating visual literacy—can be applied across the forms of writing.

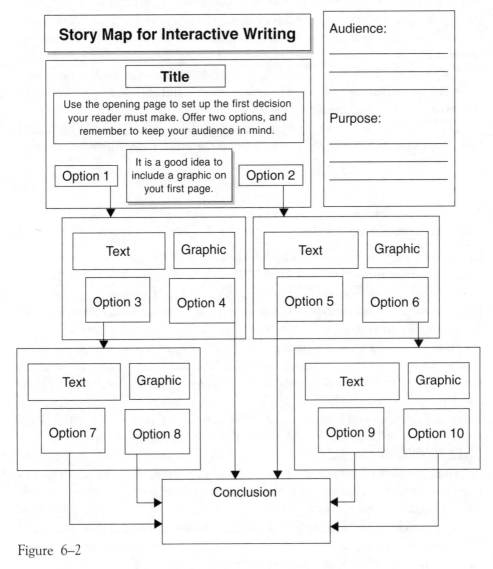

Figure 6–2

Step 2: Map It Out

Before they ever set foot in the computer lab, students should map out their stories from start to finish. The story map outline in Figure 6–2 can help them think their stories through.

When students are just beginning to write interactive stories, ask them to point all options to a single conclusion. In the interactive version of *Little Red Riding Hood,* for example, all options would conclude with the defeat of the Big Bad Wolf. Once students become comfortable with nonlinear writing, they may incorporate different conclusions.

Step 3: Add Design

Clip art and other downloaded images can enhance word-processed documents and add to the overall message of a student's writing. There are innumerable sites on the Internet that offer free downloadable clip art images. If you are using Microsoft products, the Digital Gallery Live site offers clip art, photographs, and sound clips that integrate seamlessly into the Office suite.

Students will be better able to integrate images into their work if you discuss with them some basics of design.

Images Should Complement Words

The purpose of graphic elements should be to illustrate a concept or complement the text in a specific way. I know of teachers who have students write a brief rationale for every image inserted in a piece of writing.

Before they include images, ask students to consider these questions:

1. Is this image (or other graphic element) necessary to convey my intended message?
2. Does this image or element appeal to my intended audience?
3. Does this image distract from the overall message?
4. Does this image enhance the tone I'm attempting to express?

Be sure to review with students how font styles can contribute to understanding. For example, compare Little Red Riding Hood to Little Red Riding Hood. The first example is in a font called Chiller. Ask students to predict the tone and audience of the story if it were written in that font. Now ask students to predict the tone and audience of the story if it were written in the second font, called Gigi.

Images Should Stay on the Page

Writers often make the common mistake of placing images so that they look off the page. All images should "live" within the boundaries of the page or, in the case of interactive writing, the screen. Similarly, images should not look off the page.

Larger Elements Should Be at the Top of the Page

As a general rule, larger type fonts, images, and key information—such as the title—should be at the top of the page or screen. Those who lay out newspapers call this area "above the fold." Because we read from left to right and top to bottom, we expect the important information to be bigger—and first.

Color Should Be Used Purposefully

Computers today support thousands of colors, but that doesn't mean that students should try to incorporate every shade of fuchsia into their interactive stories. As a rule of thumb, shades of red are used to emphasize key points. The eyes get tired quickly when they strain to read a lot of red. Conversely, shades of blue are easy on the eyes and convey a certain calm.

Keep Type Big and Lines Short

Because writers intend for interactive stories to be read on the computer screen, students should use a larger point size than they would when typing a traditional paper. Similarly, lines should be kept fairly short. Readers find it difficult to scan the entire width of a computer screen.

Images from the Internet: Are They Legal?

Students who download material from the Internet for educational projects are exempted from copyright restrictions if they include the following statement at the beginning of their multimedia projects: "Certain materials in this presentation are included under the fair use exemption of the U.S. Copyright Law and have been prepared with the multimedia fair use guidelines and are restricted from further use." For more on the fair use exemption clause of the U.S. Copyright Law, visit the Library of Congress Copyright Site.

Callouts and Voice Bubbles

Word-processing packages also include features that permit writers to create "auto shapes" such as callouts and discussion bubbles. Students who have trouble writing—or even those who just have trouble identifying audience—may benefit from composing stories in which conversation is set off in bubbles above a character's head. In essence, they learn to share the story first in pictures, then in text. Figure 6–3 shows the beginning of a simple story written with text boxes, discussion bubbles, and downloaded clip art.

Writing stories as comics may help to engage students who might otherwise resist putting pen to paper. The combination of words and images might help reluctant writers better communicate an overall message. In fact, some studies suggest that blending text with pictures may help children build critical reading skills and processes (Wright and Ross 1994).

Figure 6–3

Furthermore, Kylene Beers, author of *When Kids Can't Read: What Teachers Can Do*, suggests that students who have difficulty writing can benefit from sharing their stories in comics form. In a presentation at the 2002 NCTE conference, she and Linda Reif elaborated on *how* pictures help students write. The two assert that helping students learn the "language of cartooning" encourages them to see "drawing as thinking," the first step towards writing for effective communication.

Even those students who protest, "I can't draw!" can practice "thinking in pictures" by adding callouts and voice bubbles to their word-processed stories.

For more on using comics in the classroom, access the companion website. You'll find links to research articles, to the site for the National Association of Comics Art Educators, to the "Get Graphic" site at the American Library Association, and more.

Assessment

Remember what the high-school principal said at the beginning of this chapter? He associated his former English teacher with her notorious red pen. To avoid "bleeding" all over students' papers, adapt the checklist in Figure 6–4 to assess interactive stories. Access the companion website for printable checklists and links to rubric banks.

Word Processing: A Tale of Two Classrooms

Even simple projects using word-processing software can engage students in the writing process. Richard Williams is a ninth-grade English teacher at Milton High School in Alpharetta, Georgia, a school of close to 2600 students in the suburbs of Atlanta. He knows first-hand that getting students to write can be a bit, well . . . difficult. But he has found that technology can be the hook he needs to get students *involved*.

	Interactive Story Checklist	Points Possible	Points Earned: Self-Assessment	Points Earned: Teacher Assessment	Comments
1.	The story clearly presents a beginning, middle, and end.	10			
2.	The story includes at least four options for readers.	10			
3.	All options direct readers to a single conclusion.	10			
4.	The story is written for a specific audience.	10			
5.	The story has a clear purpose.	10			
6.	The story elements and options create a unified product.	10			
7.	Images and sounds are used to complement the story; they do not distract from the overall message.	10			
8.	Language used is appropriate for the audience and purpose.	10			
9.	Sentences are well constructed and mechanically correct.	10			
10.	Words are spelled correctly, and punctuation is used correctly.	10			

Figure 6–4

"The project doesn't have to be incredibly elaborate," Williams explains. "It just has to be *real*."

One such project involves simple word-processing software.

"Last spring I was teaching story writing," Williams says. "You know, we talked about plot, rising action, suspense.... To help my students really *get it*, I had them call parents of students in a second-grade class at our feeder school. My students interviewed these parents about their child's favorite TV shows, their favorite sport stars, their pets.... They then came back and wrote simple stories for each child, stories in which the child was the main character. My kids took what the parents told them and wove those elements into a story. And they had to demonstrate certain literary techniques. I told them, 'Dramatic irony, conflict . . . these things must be present.'

"Because second-graders were our audience, my students had to keep their language and sentences fairly simple. They also had to illustrate their stories with clip art that extended the message. Audience became really important. In many ways, it was the most important thing."

Williams soon discovered that students who usually groaned about writing were actually *engaged* in the process. "They were doing something for real kids," he explains. "It had to be right, and it had to be interesting."

Once Williams' students finished composing and illustrating their stories using MS Word, they printed their pages in high-resolution color and bound each book. Williams then took his students on a field trip to the elementary school where they presented the books to the second-graders. An example is shown in Figure 6–5.

"Each of my kids sat down with a second-grader. As the young kids read through the pages, they began to realize the stories were about them. They were so excited it was incredible.

"And it was a real hit with *my* kids. They worked so hard on it."

Jacob knew he had to do something to help his team, but he had already promised to be on the show. He couldn't decide what to do! Even if he decided to help his team, he had no way to get to the stadium in time! Just then, Jeff Gordon came racing up in his racecar! "Hop in," he yelled.

Figure 6–5   A page from a student word-processed storybook written and designed by one of Richard Williams' students

But the project wasn't without its complications.

"We were to begin on a Monday," Williams says. "My classroom is in a portable, and we have a wireless lab. But the weekend before we were to start there was a heavy rain that washed out our server connection. We were stuck. When we finally got that up and running, the kids couldn't find the clip art that they had saved. A lot of that had to be reloaded. But the project was worth the trouble. Everybody really had fun. The second-graders learned about reading, and my students learned about writing. Most importantly, they saw themselves as *real* writers. No amount of textbook activities could have achieved the same thing. The computer helped my students really *be* writers, editors, and publishers. When they gave the books to the second-graders, it was the icing on the cake. It really brought home the reason anyone writes: to be read."

Interactivity at Work

Violet Hopkins, a former English student teacher at Hellgate High School in Missoula, Montana, agrees that the computer and word-processing packages add a depth to student writing that would be impossible with a ballpoint pen.

"Face it," she says, "kids today are visual. They process things visually. *Seeing* an idea helps them to understand it."

To help her juniors clarify their ideas—and hence become more proficient writers—Hopkins took them to the computer lab to write their analyses of the Cormac McCarthy novel *All the Pretty Horses.*

"At first they were just typing their papers, like the computers were typewriters. They would save them up to the network so I could read their drafts. I used the "Insert Comment" feature in Word, so my comments popped up on the screen when the students accessed their papers the next day. Well, you'd have thought I waved a magic wand. The kids were all, like, 'How did you that?' When I showed them how easy it was, they wanted to know what else they could do. That's when I taught them to build bookmarks and links."

According to Hopkins, students who had previously written only superficial analyses began to look deeper into the book's themes.

"When they realized they could include hyperlinks to the Internet, they began to really examine the book's messages. For instance, one student included links to reviews of other books as he compared Cole's coming-of-age story to those of Holden Caulfield and Homer Wells from *The Cider House Rules.* What had started out as 'This book is about a boy growing up' took on new dimensions."

Hopkins says that the interactivity was mostly an afterthought, though in the future, she would incorporate it from the beginning.

"We didn't start out with storyboards or flowcharting, and that would have helped," she says. "Consequently, the papers really mushroomed, and for some students they became unwieldy. Because they could add interactivity, they made everything 'hot.' Next time I will spend more time up front focusing on audience. I hope to eventually integrate electronic portfolios into my classroom, so I can teach the students how to write formal papers that have interactive features."

Though she isn't ready to throw away notebooks and pens, Hopkins says that the computer is the communication tool students are most comfortable with.

"They're using computers for everything," she explains. "It's up to us, the teachers, to help them use computers effectively. Otherwise, they're just going to be writing in cyberslang and copying and pasting; they're not going to really *understand* anything.

"Besides, teachers are now expected to integrate technology into their lessons. In Montana, it's one of the standards teachers are evaluated on. The key is to use technology in a meaningful way. Otherwise, the kids know you're just checking off the topic on your curriculum guide. What's the point in that?"

Extending the Lesson: Scanners

Students who are already familiar with the many features of word-processing software may benefit from adding scanned pictures or documents to their writing. For example, one of my students was writing a research paper on the Plains Indians. She scanned a copy of the original treaty between the Indians and the federal government into her paper. Next to each paragraph in the treaty, she inserted comments, annotating key points that she addressed later in her analysis. She also scanned in photographs taken in the early twentieth century, and she added explanatory captions under each picture.

Of course, some students may attempt to pad their papers with irrelevant images. In fact, many teachers are afraid that students will simply copy and paste information without any true understanding. Consider setting limits to the size and number of scanned documents, and remind students to make sure that each scanned image serves to illustrate a key point. I know of teachers who ask students to always include a column of annotation next to any scanned document.

To further counter the copy-and-paste temptation, some teachers always include a presentation component to writing assignments. Students must present their work orally and be able to answer questions in order to demonstrate a comprehensive grasp of the material. Finally, any scanned document must be cited on the References page.

A caveat: Most scanners now come with Optical Content Reading (OCR) software. OCR enables scanned documents to be converted into text. For example, a student could "borrow" someone else's paper and scan it. The OCR software allows our fictitious student to open the paper in MS Word. All he has to do now is put his own name on it. Of course, students have always found ways to plagiarize. In the old days, she or he just went to the library and copied text word for word. Now the copying is easier: check out OPPapers.com, for example. Thankfully, plagiarism is also now easier to catch. If you suspect a paper has been plagiarized, type a sentence into a search engine such as Google. If the paper exists on the Internet, the search engine should find it. You can also purchase access to plagiarism-detection services such as EVE (Essay Verification Engine) and Turnitin.com. The University of Virginia distributes free antiplagiarism software on its website.

Similarly, some computer-savvy students may find it tempting to manipulate scanned images using photo-editing software. A friend related a story about a student who turned in a Hemingway assignment with an image of Papa having dinner with Britney Spears. She took it in stride because the picture was obviously faked, but it brought to her attention how easy it might be for students to reimage facts to suit themselves. As always, we teachers must rush to keep up with the students who always seem to be a step ahead of us. Perhaps this is yet another reason for us to educate ourselves about the technologies that are available.

To combat misuse of scanners and other computer equipment, some schools have instigated harsh consequences for those students who don't play by the rules. Ask your media center specialist about the Acceptable Use Policy (AUP) at your school or access the companion website for sample AUPs.

Computers are more than fancy typewriters. The tools that contemporary word processors include allow us to do so much more than simply type our papers and make easy corrections. The many features that come with word processors may serve to engage students in the writing process while reinforcing necessary—even critical—visual literacy skills. In essence, the computer may help us do what we do every day better.

7

Real Research: WebQuests

As teachers of the English language arts, we want to encourage our students to *think*. For example, when we ask them to conduct research, we want them to explore ideas, to find the joy of discovery. When the World Wide Web was just beginning its explosion, forward-thinking educators hailed it as the new frontier of learning. Finally, here was a tool that could encourage students to think critically about the world around them while they conduct meaningful—and interesting—research.

But then something happened. We typed the most innocuous keywords—like *White House*—into Internet search engines, and what the Web returned was, well, shocking. Certainly we were directed to *the* White House, but we were also directed to sites filled with pornography, racism, misinformation, and just plain errors. The Web was less an educational promise land than a dangerous, stormy sea.

To keep students safe, many of us did what any rational adult might do: We ignored the Internet.

In an Uncertain World, Why Use the Internet?

The Internet presents its fair share of dangers, but it also offers English teachers resources that can help their students respond to and analyze literature, explore history, conduct research, share ideas, and write with a real purpose for a real audience.

Imagine a typical eighth-grade classroom. Students have just read *Diary of a Young Girl,* and they're getting ready to research the Holocaust. The teacher knows the Internet would be a good resource for her students, but she's worried about asking them to conduct a search using a typical search engine or directory like Yahoo. After all, type in the word *Holocaust,* and you'll be sent to all kinds of locations. True, you'll find the United States Holocaust Memorial Museum, a site filled with educational resources, exhibits, photographs, first-person accounts, and more. But you'll also be pointed to sites that claim the Holocaust never existed, or worse yet, sites that spew out hatred and anti-Semitism.

Enter the WebQuest. A WebQuest is an inquiry-oriented activity that is teacher-directed. In essence, the teacher decides on a *path* through the Internet. The teacher preselects sites students will visit, and she or he determines what students will look for at each site. In a WebQuest, students visit specific virtual locations, find and process information, draw conclusions, and create a product—a paper, an interactive response, a video, or some other documentation of what they've learned. Oftentimes, students work on WebQuests in pairs or in small collaborative groups.

Let's go back to our imaginary eighth-grade English class. The teacher could just send students to the library to write traditional research papers. But let's face it: the static information in books and encyclopedias can distance some learners from history.

The teacher decides that a WebQuest would be a good alternative to conventional library research. She hopes that the WebQuest will *engage* students in the study of the Holocaust. Because students log on and click their way through sites, they feel empowered in their research. Further, the Internet offers quick access to multimedia resources—images, sounds, and movies—that may serve to involve reluctant learners.

All good WebQuests guide students through the completion of specific tasks. For example, some WebQuests ask students to imagine they are reporters or filmmakers or historians who must record what they "witness." In essence, students are required to take an active role in their quest, constructing their own understandings as they create an authentic record of their learning.

In this eighth-grade class, the teacher goes to the WebQuest page at San Diego State University and searches for a suitable Anne Frank quest. Once she finds one that includes the research information she wants her students to access, the teacher directs her class to an Anne Frank WebQuest; in this case, she sends her students to a site developed by English education students at Florida State University. The WebQuest, titled *Anne Frank: A Timeline Adventure*, takes students back in time to report on Anne Frank's life and the Holocaust experience. Students are told to imagine they are journalists for an international magazine, *Time Line*, and their assignment is to complete two specific tasks that take them on a virtual tour through the experiences of Anne Frank. For each undertaking, students write their impressions, document eyewitness accounts, and respond to images, sounds, and videos in a "travel diary."

Students are guided on their journey by a set of questions the "editor" of *Time Line* magazine has assigned. The questions ask students to record what they discover, respond to what they read, and sort through their own emotions. For example, the first time-travel experience takes students back to 1942, the year Anne and her family move into the secret annex. The students investigate and answer questions that guide them from simple recall to synthesis.

The WebQuest then provides links to three Anne Frank Internet sites that have been evaluated for appropriateness and accuracy. Students "journey" through the sites, exploring the issues and events that lead up to the Frank family's capture. As they move from site to site, students copy and paste pictures of Anne and of the secret annex into their electronic travel diaries, and they reflect—in writing—on their expedition.

Students then "transport" to more generalized Holocaust sites. The Quest guides students from an understanding of the specifics surrounding Anne and her family to a consideration of the Holocaust in full. In this way, they begin to see that what happened to Anne and her family was only one part of a greater evil.

Because WebQuests are inquiry driven, students wrestle with the "big questions." In this case, students consider the weighty issue of genocide, an issue critical in the face of so-called "ethnic cleansings" in Bosnia, Sudan, and elsewhere. Because sites on the Internet can be updated frequently, the WebQuest can stay timely by relating the big questions to the events of the day. In this way, students see the explicit connection between content studied in class and the world around them.

The Quest then takes students on an emotionally evocative tour of Auschwitz, where Anne was sent after her discovery in the annex. Students explore historical documents and photographs and are asked to consider what Anne might have written in her diary had she been permitted to keep one at the camp. Students are thus asked to empathize with Anne—and with the other prisoners in the camp.

To compare the worst of human nature with the best, the WebQuest directs students in an exploration of the lives of such heroes of the time as Oskar Schindler and Raoul Wallenberg. The Quest helps students connect these historical figures to their own lives by asking them to imagine how they might have helped those who were being targeted by the Nazis.

The WebQuest doesn't just take students into the past; it brings them back to the present by directing them to a site of Holocaust art created by contemporary artists. Students are asked to decide on captions for the artwork by selecting and applying quotations from *Diary of a Young Girl*. In essence, students discover not only the historical episodes of the past, they learn how the lessons of the Holocaust are relevant in their lives today.

At the conclusion of the WebQuest, students decide how they want to publish their timeline diaries. They may post their work on the Web, they may create a class newsletter, or they may display their most prized responses on a traditional classroom corkboard. As a result of this WebQuest, students discover the wealth of the Internet without being subjected to its hidden—or not so hidden—dangers. They become *involved* with the material; after all, they aren't merely students conducting research, they are journalists on a quest.

One of the key tenets of constructivism holds that students create their own knowledge by relating new concepts to what they already understand. In the example above, our imaginary group of eighth-graders related what they discovered about genocide to the story of Anne Frank and, in turn, to their own lives. Further, they explored the "big questions" in a variety of ways. Students wrote, they talked, and they created art. At the end of the project, they published a product, a learning artifact that demonstrated authentic engagement.

In summary, a WebQuest is an inquiry-oriented project that directs students to explore the Internet while they complete specific tasks. It *involves* students in research by asking them to assume a role, document their findings, and draw conclusions. A WebQuest capitalizes on the sounds, words, and images of the Internet to engage students in their learning in an interesting and meaningful way. Finally, it provides a safe alternative to sending students blindly into the murky world of cyberspace.

Getting Started

One of the best ways to find out if a WebQuest is right for your students is to complete one yourself. The WebQuest page at San Diego State University—*the* authoritative WebQuest site—provides a number of "WebQuests about WebQuests" to help educators explore the concept and decide whether it would be useful in their teaching.

At the San Diego State University WebQuest site, you can investigate many language arts-related WebQuests that have already been prepared by practicing and preservice teachers. For example, one project takes students on an exploration of censorship as part of the study of Bradbury's *Fahrenheit 451*. Another guides learners through an "E-Gallery" of tragic heroes from literature and life. Yet another asks them to extend the ending of *The Giver*.

You may also find existing WebQuests by conducting a keyword search in a search engine such as AltaVista or Lycos. A search for *anne frank webquest* returned more than twenty pages of related materials; some are, of course, better than others. You can also find WebQuests on such education sites as Ozline.com, DiscoverySchool.com, Global Schoolhouse, Education World, and TeachersFirst.com. See this book's website for up-to-date links.

For the most part, WebQuests are modeled on the same template, so students who engage in one Quest quickly become familiar with the process. WebQuests include six major sections:

1. **Introduction** The introduction hooks the learner by establishing the situation, offering background information, and posing a question or presenting a problem.
2. **Task** The task gives a brief overview of what students are to do. It outlines clearly what the end result of the Quest will be: a paper, a multimedia project, a bulletin board, or so on.
3. **Process** The process section describes the steps of the WebQuest; it explains roles and clarifies each part of the assignment. This section includes links to supporting Internet resources. It is critical that students are not left to wander aimlessly about the Net.
4. **Evaluation** This section specifies how participation will be assessed. Often the evaluative part of a WebQuest contains a rubric or mastery checklist.
5. **Conclusion** The conclusion section reiterates major themes of the WebQuest and poses additional questions for reflection.
6. **Teacher Page** This section includes information to help other teachers implement the Quest. Here you will find such things as goals and objectives, teaching notes, and examples of student projects.

Adapting Existing Quests

Some WebQuests may not *exactly* meet your needs. For instance, you might think that a Quest contains good information and directs students to safe and interesting sites. However, you may believe that the questions included aren't constructivist in nature, or you may find that they don't address key points you've discussed in class. It isn't possible to edit Quests online; such changes would interfere with the designer's vision for the Quest—and would be akin to colorizing classic black-and-white movies. However, feel free to adapt an assignment to meet the specific needs of your students by creating your own Quest based on preexisting ones, or by simply distributing copies of an addendum. Write your own questions, add new sites, delete or modify projects, or add vocabulary "cheat sheets." WebQuests on the Internet are intended for educators to use as they see fit. In a way, these projects exemplify the original promise of the Web: a free and useful exchange of ideas.

Designing Your Own WebQuest

Teachers who use WebQuests in their classrooms and see firsthand the excitement such projects engender often feel compelled to design their own. But they may worry that creating and publishing a Quest is something only geeks can do. Not so. If you have access to a computer, you can design your own WebQuest quickly, easily, and for free.

Again, one of the best places to start is the San Diego WebQuest page. You can access a downloadable template that directs you, step by step, through the process of creating a WebQuest. Save the template to your hard drive and complete each section as directed. The first screen, for example, instructs you to "Put the Title of the Lesson Here."

The template available on the San Diego University site is by no means the only one available. The Web is filled with sites that will help you create and post your own WebQuests. You don't even need to know any special computer-ese like Hypertext Markup Language (HTML), and you don't need to know how to use a Web editor like Microsoft's FrontPage. If you can fill in the blanks, you can create an engaging WebQuest and put it on the Internet. An Internet search will yield any number of sites that offer no-cost hosting to teachers and many provide easy-to-follow tutorials for putting material online. To build links in one such site,

teachers need only complete a chart similar to this one:

Location:	http://
Title:	
Description: (Optional)	

WebQuests in the Classroom

Cindy Adams teaches sophomore and junior English at Vestavia Hills High School in Birmingham, Alabama. She designed a World War I WebQuest to help

her tenth-grade students prepare to read *All Quiet on the Western Front*. The project is accessible from the Vestavia Hills High School site.

"I use WebQuests because I try to use constructivist approaches to learning," Adams explains. "Instead of teacher lectures, the WebQuests allow the students to discover essential information on their own, supported by the structure of the WebQuest. I use WebQuests primarily before we begin study and reading of a new novel. They help provide the background knowledge students need to better comprehend the novel's setting, characters, and themes, which in turn helps students maintain motivation to read."

In the introduction to the WWI quest, Adams informs her students that they are a carefully chosen group of soldiers who will act covertly to gather information for Kaiser Wilhelm's Secret Service. They are to gather information that will either confirm or disprove information already flowing into the kaiser's staff office.

The task specifies that a deputy in the kaiser's office has given each student a piece of paper with "hastily scrawled questions" on it. Students are to answer the questions as completely as possible in the time available. Questions and answers are to be written in a "trench journal."

A link takes students to a screen with the questions. The screen reads:

Dear Comrade,

Please be careful and work quickly to find out the answers to the following questions:

1. Many new weapons are being used in this Great War. Explain what the following are in 2–3 sentences each and tell how they are changing warfare: flamethrower, tank, machine gun, submarine, airplane, 3-inch mortar.
2. What does the phrase "no-man's-land" mean?
3. Why does gas warfare draw so much attention? Explain the types used and their effects.
4. What is life like for a soldier in the trenches on the Western Front?
5. What types of food do soldiers often have to eat in the trenches when they can't move behind the fighting lines to get to the military kitchens? Find a recipe for a dish the soldiers might make.
6. The Red Baron makes all of Germany proud. Who is he? What makes him so good? How many enemy aircraft does he shoot down? How does he finally die?
7. Explain the Schlieffen Plan. Is it working in 1917?
8. How did the war start? What assassination started it officially?
9. Who is Helen Burrey? What does her journal talk about in 1917?
10. What is a dogfight in military terms of World War I?
11. Sketch a typical trench in your journal. Look below for a good example or watch for drawings and photos of trenches during your quest on the Web.

Adams then provides links to relevant sites, a conclusion, and evaluation criteria. In addition to writing their responses, students select pictures, illustrations, and diagrams to print out and paste in their "trench journals."

"The students engage with WebQuests," Adams says, "and active learning happens. I've been pleased with the retention of knowledge after the students work on WebQuests. I think the best ones are the ones a teacher custom-fits for use in his or her particular classes."

If you decide to use WebQuests in your classroom, consider adapting the assessment rubric shown in Figure 7–1 to meet your specific needs. You can download a printable version from this book's companion website.

Extending the Lesson: Student-generated Quests

Students who are already familiar with the format of WebQuests may benefit from designing and publishing their own Quests. After all, teaching others is a good way to solidify one's own conceptual understanding. Further, asking students to design and create their own WebQuests may serve to "spark the imagination, solve problems, and promote discussion about important issues" (Yoder 1999, 53). And remember that you don't need to post a Quest to the Internet for it to have value. You can upload student-generated Quests to your classroom hard disk, to the network drive in your school's lab, or to your district's Intranet.

To help your students design their own WebQuests, guide them through these steps:

1. **The big question**   Identify one or two "big questions" on which to focus. For example, if your students have just finished reading *The Cay*, they may want to question how "seeing" may interfere with true understanding.
2. **The theme**   Decide upon a theme that extends the "big question." Students building a Quest based on the question in step 1, for example, may decide on a theme of racism.
3. **The scenario**   Have students devise a scenario that will serve to communicate the mission of the Quest. For example: *Imagine you are a reporter covering the civil rights movement. Travel from place to place recording what occurs. Summarize what you "witness" and share the lessons you learn in a letter to Phillip* (the boy in *The Cay*).
4. **The sites**   Have students find three or four appropriate websites to serve as links on the Quest. If you're hesitant about sending them onto the Web, Education World offers safe Internet searching, as does Yahooligans. Remember that sites often go down, so ask students to include only established Internet locations, such as the site maintained by National Civil Rights Museum. To ensure accuracy, suggest that students avoid sites created by individuals and posted on public arenas such as Geocities.

5. **The questions** Students should devise a series of higher-level questions to accompany each stage of the Quest. Suggest that they develop questions that ask visitors to explore an issue from another point of view or that ask for a decision.

6. **The Assessment** Ask students to create a checklist or rubric that will ensure that the Quest has been completed successfully. Consider having students adapt the rubric included in Figure 7–1.

7. **Reflection** Students should include a section that encourages visitors to reflect on what they learned as a result of the Quest. For example, they may wish to have students draw a poster that exemplifies the themes of the Quest.

The WebQuest is a valuable teaching and learning tool that capitalizes on the timely resources of the Internet in a safe and engaging way. One of my former student teachers once told me that the hardest thing about WebQuests was limiting students to their assigned roles. "They want to do all the parts," he said.

	Outstanding 4 points	Excellent 3 points	Good 2 points	Completed 1 point	Not Completed 0 points	Total Points
Mechanics of written work	All written work is turned in on time with no grammatical errors or miss-pellings.	All written work is turned in on time with few minor errors in grammar or spelling.	All written work is turned in on time. Several errors in grammar or spelling.	All written work is completed; however, it may not have been turned in on time, and/or there are numerous errors in grammar or spelling.	Written work was not turned in.	
Conceptual under-standing as demon-strated in written work	You have a clear understanding of the information you researched. You can explain thoroughly the Who, What, When, Where, Why and How of your research.	You have a good under-standing of information you researched, but your explanation of the Who, What, When, Where, Why, and How lacks coherence or specifics.	You have an initial under-standing of the information you researched, but your explanation of the Who, What, When, Where, Why, and How contains errors.	You are only able to explain one or two key elements of your research and/or your work was not done within the allotted time frame.	Understanding was not communicated.	
Collaborative work	Completes all individual tasks for the group on time and with quality; partici-pates in a constructive manner and shares responsi-bility.	Completes all individual tasks for the group on time and with quality, but participation is not always constructive.	Completes all individual tasks for the group on time and with quality. Group interaction is often negative.	Completes all individual tasks for the group, but did not complete on time or with complete quality and/or group interaction was destructive.	Did not complete individual tasks and/or did not work with group.	
Oral presenta-tion of project	Engages audience in presentation by demonstrating enthusiasm for the topic, using oral language well (vocal qualities), using body language effectively (eye contact, posture, gestures), asking questions of the audience, and responding well to questions.	Attempts to engage audience in presentation; use of oral and body language is good overall, but not consistent (fits and starts, staring at notes, muttering); does not ask questions of the audience, but responds well to questions.	Attempts to engage audience in presentation, but does not make good use of oral and body language. Responds to questions well overall, but must refer to notes.	Does not attempt to engage audience in presentation. Information is read from notes. Does not answer questions, or answers questions incorrectly.	Project was not presented.	

© 2003 by Hilve Firek from *Ten Easy Ways to Use Technology in the English Classroom*. Portsmouth, NH: Heinemann.

Figure 7–1

8

Organizing Ideas: Concept-Mapping Software

At some point or other, I'm sure you've heard a student or two say something like "I just don't get it."

Quite often, this statement comes as a surprise. After all, we are caring, knowledgeable teachers who practice the best constructivist practices and who ask students to participate in meaningful class activities. Sometimes it seems as if we devote every waking moment to helping students "get it."

Still, no matter how hard we try we try to make content relevant, students inevitably get lost. It may be because they're thinking about more important things—like the prom or the upcoming football game. It may also be because they have trouble organizing information in meaningful ways.

Key to critical thinking is the ability to distinguish between important and irrelevant facts. In order to *learn*, students need to be able to prioritize information and organize concepts—especially if they expect to do well on the myriad of standardized tests thrust upon them. Those students who have trouble distinguishing between relevant and extraneous information may find success in school elusive, especially if that success is based solely on an end-of-course test.

Let me share an example. Several years ago I taught a unit on the Holocaust to a class of ninth graders. We spent several weeks reviewing the history of Europe prior to World War II. We read and discussed first-person accounts of survivors. We acted out—Readers' Theater style—the play version of *Anne Frank* that was in our textbooks. We watched and responded to excerpts from documentaries. I truly thought all the students were engaged.

Then one day, at the beginning of class, I asked students to respond in their journals to the following prompt: "Imagine this classroom is World War II Germany. Would you rather be a Nazi or a Jew? Why?" Most students began writing in earnest, but one young man raised his hand.

"Which ones got beaten up again?"

I had made a critical error. At no time in the weeks of study had I asked students to organize, in their own words, the information covered in the unit. This student had dutifully participated in the activities, but in his mind, distinguishing between Nazis and Jews was no different than identifying what color smock Anne Frank was wearing the day she was captured. Had I asked students earlier to organize key ideas, he might have better understood what was important and what was not. At the very least, I would have noticed that he was having trouble identifying critical relationships.

Concept Mapping: Why Bother?

One way to help students organize their ideas is to have them create a concept map, a visual representation of their understanding. Because so many young people are visual—they think in pictures—asking them to create an image-rich diagram of relationships may help them work through their ideas and organize their thoughts.

According to Linda Lohr (2003), visual learners process information in hierarchies of groups, or chunks. Hierarchies communicate the importance of ideas by the way they are displayed. In other words, visual learners tend to stratify information in layers or different levels. Hierarchies provide a path by which visual learners make meaning (203).

Asking students to map out their thoughts helps them to understand how ideas are connected. Further, organizing ideas in a graphical format helps students simplify difficult concepts. In essence, graphic organizers encourage students to arrange new ideas in relation to previously learned concepts, thus reinforcing what has already been studied.

Robert J. Marzano calls visual learning tools, such as graphic organizers, "nonlinguistic representations" (2000, 69). Because much of what happens in school is linguistic—we talk about ideas or we read about them—visual students may misunderstand key ideas or misinterpret relationships. When teachers *guide* students in creating visual representations, Marzano suggests, achievement increases. The fundamental principle behind the effective use of graphic organizers is that students *develop* new knowledge; they don't simply restate what the teacher says. Perhaps Jim Burke states the rationale for using graphic organizers best: "Kids cannot read or write about what they cannot understand, and they cannot understand what they cannot 'see'" (2002, *xx*).

As English teachers, we are very comfortable with words. We are, perhaps, less comfortable with images. Luckily, there are a number of computer programs that may help ease us into the world of "nonlinguistic representations."

Concept-mapping Software: Using the Computer to Organize Ideas

Of course, students who have difficulty understanding concepts are often the same ones who associate schoolwork with drudgery. Drawing a traditional concept map means putting pen to paper, and revising means drawing the whole thing over again.

Software programs such as *Inspiration* may help take some of the toil out of designing concept maps. Software helps students organize their ideas visually, with colorful and engaging graphics that come preloaded or that can be downloaded from the Internet. Easy-to-use electronic graphic organizers encourage productive thinking by bringing order to concepts and by providing a visual reference for abstract ideas. For example, the simple character map in Figure 8–1 was created by a student in *Inspiration*. Not only are ideas organized into a structure a student can *see*, the downloaded images serve as visual mnemonic devices.

Inspiration comes preloaded with templates for character analysis, vocabulary, story maps, and more. Struggling students may like the format of the templates, whereas more advanced students may prefer creating their own graphic organizers. Whether students work from templates or not, the process of creating a graphic organizer demands that they *reimagine* their ideas.

Graphic Organizers for Prereading and Reading

In addition to helping students order information, graphic organizers illustrate the patterns and relationships among ideas. Further, they can stimulate creative thinking by prompting students to think of relationships that may not be obvious. Brainstorming, for example, is particularly well suited to graphic organizing software. *Inspiration* includes what it calls a "rapid fire" feature that encourages students to get their ideas down quickly. Figure 8–2 shows a two-minute brainstorm around the idea of *tragedy*.

This brainstorm was used as a prereading activity for *Romeo and Juliet*. It helped students clarify, in their own minds, the characteristics of tragedy. Further,

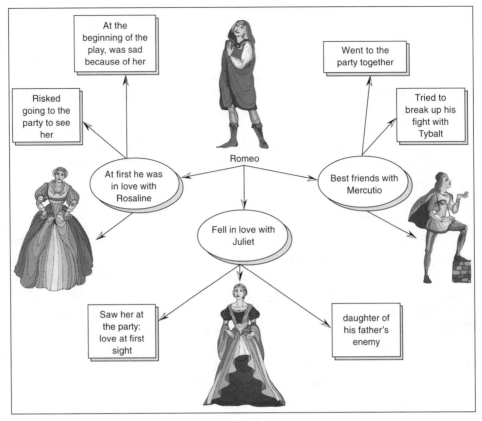

Figure 8–1

it helped the teacher identify misconceptions: not all tragedies involve unrequited love, for example. As students learn new information, they can update and revise the map to reflect new understandings. Maintaining a concept map throughout a unit of study encourages reflection and self-correction, and because revision is easy on the computer, students begin to see learning as something that changes and grows.

Graphic Organizers for Prewriting

Many teachers use concept maps to help students organize ideas before they begin the writing process. To help students begin a concept map, ask them to identify the main idea around which they will work. A student working on a typical writing assignment may start with something like "Our summer trip to Nags Head."

Once a student has identified a main idea, ask him or her to brainstorm questions pertaining to the topic. For a trip to Nags Head, the student might ask, "How did we get there?" "Where did we stay?" "What did we do?" From

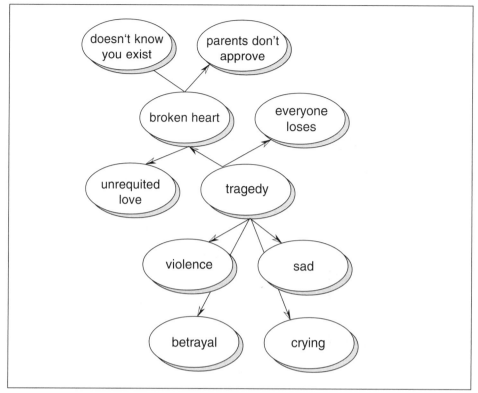

Figure 8–2

there, the concept map begins to take shape. Any difficulties in organization can be addressed before students even begin composing a rough draft. Take a look at the prewriting map in Figure 8–3, for example. The student is beginning to organize ideas around topics and the graphics serve as visual cues, but there are a few issues the teacher may wish to address before the actual composing process begins.

For instance, the teacher might want to ask the student to elaborate on his comment that the restaurant was "yucky." What made it yucky? The food? The atmosphere? Also, what kind of "place" did they stay in? A cottage? A beachfront condo? And the fact that the student wrote that he missed his friend Chuck is an interesting detail, but it doesn't belong under the topic "Where did we stay?"

Once these issues are discussed and resolved, the student begins to "see" her ideas on paper. She can then use the graphic organizer as a roadmap for creating a cohesive essay. The main idea becomes the introductory paragraph, and the supporting ideas become the body of the composition. In fact, the very idea of paragraph cohesion may be easier for students once they can *see* their ideas organized on a map. And revising an electronic map may be easier for students than rewriting a rough draft.

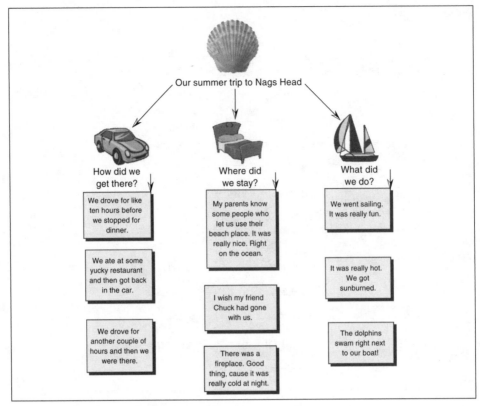

Figure 8–3

In essence, students process their ideas in nonlinguistic ways *before* they begin formal writing. The visual steps inherent in creating a graphic organizer encourage the reimagining of ideas. Students integrate new knowledge by "chunking" it into hierarchies and representing it pictorially. They establish relationships and connections, and they begin to see how ideas may be structured. Bottom line: Asking students to take the structure of the organizer and apply it to the writing process may help them find success. And such successes may even translate into greater achievement on the many writing tests students are asked to complete (Marzano 2000).

Graphic Organizing Software and "Media Memory": One Teacher's Experience

Elaine Simos regularly uses *Inspiration* with her eleventh-grade students at Downers Grove North High School, a school of 2100 students in the Chicago suburb of Downers Grove.

"I use *Inspiration* all the time," Simos says. "I have my students use it to create concept maps for all kinds of content reasons. . . . I ask kids to create organizers for almost everything. If we're doing character analysis, I ask them to make a map. Literary analysis? Make a map."

Simos can't hide the enthusiasm in her voice. In her experience, students actually learn more when they create graphic organizers.

"They can articulate their ideas better," she explains. "*Inspiration* gives them practice working with concepts, with their thoughts. They can *see* connections."

Simos finds that using *Inspiration* taps into what she calls "media memory."

"We're all so visual," she explains. "Using graphic organizers on the computer is easy, and students can *picture* the ideas. The images are already there in their minds; they've seen a lot of movies and they've watched a lot of television. *Inspiration* helps them recall that media memory and apply it to the concepts we're studying in class."

Simos thinks that students at all levels can benefit from using electronic organizers.

"With lower-level students, I often collect the maps to check for understanding and then redistribute them when it's time to write an essay. This way the students have the material ready and organized for their writing . . . with some tweaking if needed. With higher-level students, I have them check each other's maps. They get the practice putting their ideas in visual terms, and they get practice checking how other students have pictured the same ideas. The learning is reinforced on so many levels."

According to Simos, asking students to organize their ideas ahead of time pays off when it's time to begin writing.

"The students tend to create more organized essays when they have the opportunity to use these maps," she says. "They seem to understand even complex concepts more thoroughly and with more investiture in the ideas since they've worked with them so much."

Further, Simos believes students are more enthusiastic about writing when they begin with the visual images they can incorporate with *Inspiration*. "There doesn't seem to be as much griping," she says, laughing. "Since we've been using the computer's graphic organizing software, students know that writing is something they can be successful with. They know that they'll have the chance to interact with their ideas before committing them to paper."

Simos knows that some teachers may think creating nonlinguistic representations takes up too much time in a schedule already pushed to the limit. But she considers creating graphic organizers time well spent.

"I've found that it's better to spend time up-front," she says, "when you can help students correct any misunderstandings. Once they've written an essay, it's hard to get them to go back and revisit their ideas. And it's hard to get them to 'unlearn' something they've misunderstood."

In essence, Simos is sold on the benefits of visual organizers.

"It may seem like a really simple thing," she says. "But it's the simple things that work best. All I can tell you is that this easy little computer program has made a big difference in how my kids write and how they learn."

Assessing Understanding

 Encourage your students to review their own concept maps using the checklist in Figure 8–4. Once they have assessed their own work, review the maps and checklists to determine where students need help. A printable form is available for download on the companion website. Adapt this form to meet your own needs.

Extending the Lesson: Creating an Electronic Library of Graphic Organizers

Needless to say, students perform better when they are working for real reasons and real audiences. Once students master graphic organizer software, ask them to create templates for English activities that can be stored on disk or on your school's network. These templates can be accessed by students in other classes or by future students. For example, consider having students build an electronic library of templates for prereading, prewriting, brainstorming, identifying similarities and differences, organizing related concepts, and more.

You can also ask students to create electronic organizers for each literary piece read in class. At the end of a semester, they have visual outlines of every story—the perfect study aid for end-of-course exams!

Concept Map Checklist	✓
The main idea is clearly identified.	
Relationships are signaled by descriptive words.	
Images clearly illustrate an idea or concept.	
Ideas are organized appropriately.	
Concepts are supported with concrete examples.	
The map presents a coherent idea.	
Details are explicit.	

Figure 8–4

9

All the World's Your Classroom: Creating a Class Website

We've heard the message time and again: The Internet will change the way teachers teach and students learn. But is that actually happening? More important, *can* it happen?

Creating a Website: Why Bother?

Reading, writing, speaking, and listening: These are the hallmarks of an English classroom. But the Internet? Where does it *fit*?

To identify the role of the Net in the English classroom, many teachers point to its wealth of resources. For example, students can find full-text copies of thousands of books in the public domain at Project Gutenberg. Similarly, they can search encyclopedias, dictionaries, and academic databases.

But the potential contribution of the Internet to teaching and learning extends beyond its function as a virtual library. The Internet is, at its heart, a community. It gathers together those who think alike—and those who vehemently disagree. It welcomes all opinions equally, no matter how enlightened or repugnant. It offers you—and your students—a place to publish writing and to discuss ideas with people who live on the other side of the globe. With today's Web translation features, people can converse with one another without even speaking the same language.

But if students are to participate fully in this new community, they must have integral skills at hand, skills that should look very familiar to English teachers: "critical thinking, problem-solving, written communication, and the ability to work collaboratively'" (Owston 1997, 31).

Creating a class Web page can help your students hone the skills necessary in today's point-and-click world. For example, the Net is still primarily text-based; therefore, a student needs to be able to write effectively. But teaching writing has always been one of the more difficult of an English teacher's countless jobs. Publishing student writing on the Internet may be able to help. After all, "writing to an authentic audience—rather than only to the teacher—has long been viewed as critical for the development of students' writing ability" (Owston, 31). Of course, a class website provides students the opportunity to do just that.

Further, because the Web is a multimedia tool, students may include a variety of resources in their projects: sound files, pictures, graphics, animation, and video clips, to name a few. Asking students to create a cohesive product using a number of elements encourages them to make evaluative decisions, structure their work effectively, and select media that bests communicates their message.

In essence, your class website can be a virtual publishing center, a communications area, a homework zone, and an electronic library. Together, the Web provides opportunities for learning unlike any other.

But Don't I Have to Know Computer Stuff?

Back in the day, only those privileged few who knew HyperText Markup Language (HTML) could create Web pages. But now, if you can fill in the blanks, you can put the interactivity of the Web to work for your students.

One of the easiest and fastest ways to get content on the Web is to access a template program, such as the Web Wizard Worksheet hosted by the University of Kansas. See Figure 9–1. You can find other free hosting sites for teachers by doing a keyword search in an engine such as Google, or by accessing this book's companion website.

Once you choose from the predesigned formats, the template prompts you to fill in the blanks with the information you want to put on the Web. You can insert pictures, resources, and information selected to meet your students' specific needs.

The University of Kansas also hosts Project Poster, a website wizard for student projects. Students share their work with the world by simply selecting a design and inserting the text and photos from their projects or reports. Student pages remain active—or live—for one month.

If your school has its own server, you can create a page for it using the Homepage Maker at Teachers.net. As with the previous tools, you just insert your information in the blanks, select colors, clip art, and a background, and click Create It!

The important difference between Teachers.net and the previous sites mentioned is that Teachers.net does not host your site. You must request that the page be emailed to you . . . or to your school's technology coordinator. Once you have the page, you can forward it to your school's webspinner, the person who manages and updates your school's site. The advantage is that parents and students can access your page directly from your school's site; they don't need to remember a different Web address in order to download a homework assignment or to see what's on the schedule.

Getting Organized

To get the most out of your class website, you might want to turn to the ADDIE model of instructional design (Lohr 2003, 282–83):

- **Analysis** Begin by analyzing and identifying your instructional goals. What is it you hope students will gain by having access to a class Web site? Do you want them to publish the drafts of their writing? Or only their final products? Do you want them to communicate with peers? Do you want them to create their own specific Web pages?

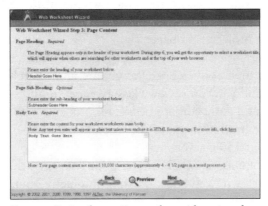

Figure 9–1   http://wizard.org/thewizard

- **Design** Write your performance goals. Determine, with your students, what they already know how to do and what they hope to learn. Outline the format of the class website. What will it look like? What functionality will it include?
- **Development** Gather resources, engage students in writing new content, and insert materials into a Web page template. To encourage visual literacy skills, consider asking students to take digital pictures or to scan photographs to include on the site.
- **Implementation** Once your website is developed, put it on the Net. (By the way, the day a site is activated is called its "go live" date.) Don't worry if the site isn't perfect. One of the terrific things about the Web is that you can correct mistakes and change content whenever you want. Furthermore, students can bring down their old projects and improve them whenever they wish. Consequently, revision has real value; it's no longer just an academic exercise.
- **Evaluation.** A website is under constant scrutiny. If something doesn't look quite right, rest assured that someone will let you know. Similarly, if your website is difficult to navigate, you will hear about it. Involve students in evaluating the class website and their own pages on it. The checklist in Figure 9–2 may offer some ideas.

Online Activity Sites

You can find any number of subscription services for teachers on the Web. One of the best is Quia.com

Quia is a *very* user-friendly site with lots of interactive features you can customize for your students. For example, you can create a concentration-style game for a test review, hangman games for vocabulary, cloze exercises, and other things to post on your website. You can also create your own password-protected page so that only your students and parents can access your information. Of course, you can also upload student projects and papers.

The interactive quiz feature allows you to post quizzes and tests online so students can take them at their convenience. Scores are immediately transferred to your Quia gradebook, and you can review class averages, most frequently missed questions, and other useful data. Perhaps best of all, students get immediate feedback: no more waiting until you grade the papers and pass them back. At present, Quia costs about $50 per year.

MySchoolOnline.com is another subscription service that guides you through setting up your own Web page, creating interactive quizzes, and maintaining an electronic gradebook. It, too, permits you to post student work online. It currently runs about $30 per year.

Using Checklists to Guide Your Students' Web pages

Encouraging students to view the Internet with a critical eye is one of the most important tasks of today's teachers. Just as we instruct students to not believe everything they read, so too must we guide them in discovering what is accurate—and what is not—on the World Wide Web.

You can find scores of critical evaluation instruments on the Net. The following checklist, based on Yahooligan's *4 A's*, adapts an evaluation instrument for use in designing an effective website. Use it to help guide your students in the creation of their own Web pages, and adapt it as you need to for use with other sites.

Access the companion website for a printable version of this form. Also, find links to other critical evaluation tools you can use in your classroom.

Empowering Every Student with the Web: A CyberEnglish Story

Ted Nellen started teaching English in 1974. Ten years later, something happened that would forever change the way he perceived teaching and learning. He took a job in a New York City high school; in his classroom was a computer.

"Actually, I'd always been interested in technology," Nellen explained, "even before we had computers. I took a bookbinding class in college. What the professor wanted to do was to introduce us, as writers, to the idea of having control over the entire publishing environment. He said that writers were perhaps the only artists who don't have control over their product, unlike dancers or painters. Writers create something, and then they turn it over to editors and publishers, and often the product changes.

"So in this bookbinding class, we wrote our own poetry, and then we selected the font faces and ink colors and the paper. We made and bound the books, and then we distributed them. We took them to an area bookstore; I sold three of the five books I wrote."

Nellen said that being in control of the writing process from the formation of the initial idea to final publication harked back to the spirit of Martin Luther who nailed his ninety-five theses on the church door in Wittenburg, and to Ben Franklin who ran his own printing press.

"I guess in its simplest form, it's the power of 'he who owns the press,'" Nellen said. "I really felt that then."

But students in English classes rarely felt that power or that control, Nellen explained.

"What teachers do, traditionally, is they take the good work and put it on the wall," he said. "It's a nice concept, but it's rarely ever read, and it's the teacher who's choosing what goes up. Schools have literary magazines and such, but they have limited publication. Not everyone participates."

✓	**Checklist for Developing Websites** **Based on Yahooligan's *4 A's:* Accessible, Accurate,** **Appropriate, and Appealing**
Is the site accessible?	
	Does it load quickly? (If not, cut down on the size or number of graphics.)
	Can visitors find their way around easily? (If not, make navigation buttons or links more prominent.)
	Do all the links work? (If not, replace them with new ones.)
	Is a webspinner email address included? (If not, add one at the bottom of the opening screen.)
	If users need plug-ins (e.g., Flash, QuickTime), are links to the download sites readily available?
Is the site accurate?	
	Can visitors tell who is responsible for the information? (If not, be sure there is a statement identifying this site as student-generated.)
	Can visitors easily identify the educational affiliation of the site? (If not, include a link to your school's main page.)
	Are sources of information identified and cited properly? (If not, check an MLA style manual for help.)
Is the site appropriate?	
	Is the site appropriate for its intended audience? (If not, reconsider word choice and design.)
Is the site appealing?	
	Are layout and design pleasing? (If not, reconsider color and graphics)
	Is text on the screen easy to read? (If not, increase point size and switch to a sans serif font.)
© 2003 by Hilve Firek from *Ten Easy Ways to Use Technology in the English Classroom.* Portsmouth, NH: Heinemann.	

Figure 9–2

Encouraging all students to view themselves as writers has been a lifelong goal, Nellen said.

"We write for a number of reasons," he said. "We write to be read, and we write to learn what we know. But kids weren't writing to be read. They were writing for the teacher, and just having a teacher do the reading isn't good enough."

Consequently, Nellen relied on whatever technology was available at the time—carbon paper, mimeograph machines—so that his students could share their work with each other. When computers came on the scene, he realized that students could write for a worldwide audience. They could, in essence, have access to the same power Ben Franklin had.

"Immediately, with gopher servers—the technology we had back then—I could put student work up on the Internet so that the kids could do peer review," Nellen said. "Then something really cool happened. People from the outside started visiting the site, and they saw what these kids did, and they began writing to them about their work. The immediate result was telementors."

Telementors are adults in the community who agree to exchange emails with students. The telementors guide students in their writing and in other academic endeavors.

"I find that telementors come from all walks of life," Nellen said. "They are retirees, college students, alumni, military people, and even other teachers. One of the best by-products has been students communicating with their parents via email. Parents are able to view their child's websites, see their work, comment on it, and become engaged with their child's education."

Some may wonder about the risks of telementoring. After all, many of these virtual mentors are not teachers. But the *realness* of the exchanges more than makes up for any lack of professional training.

"It's the masses educating the masses," Nellen said. "Utilizing the human resources of the country . . . the world . . ., educators can now provide all kinds of knowledge to their students. Pedagogy will not be compromised, it will be enhanced."

Because students correspond with people from outside the school, Nellen makes sure they understand Internet safety issues.

"I tell them, 'If someone says something that makes you uncomfortable, click him off and let me know.' I tell them, 'Never meet anyone, no matter how nice they may seem.' I really believe the Internet is safer than walking down the street. If the student doesn't like a message, he can just delete it."

The practical benefits of a website for student work are more numerous than one can imagine, Nellen said.

"Let's say a teacher has 150 kids; how does an English teacher grade that many essays every weekend? A typical essay demands fifteen to twenty minutes of a teacher's time. Do the math. You're looking at forty hours of reading. What I did was this: I had my students publish their work on the Web. While they are writing, I can go online and see exactly where they are. I can monitor what each student is doing. I could then go over to a particular student who needs help, or if I see a number of people making a mistake—or doing something good—I can put it up on the projector, and we can talk about it. There's my lesson right there. If they're going in the wrong direction, I can nip it in the bud. I'm involved with them *during* the writing process. I can actually go into each computer and watch each student type. It's almost like brain surgery; I can watch each student *think*."

Nellen also pushed his students to value their own opinions—and those of their classmates.

"My students engaged in a lot of peer review," he said. "I told them, 'I want you to talk with each other. Have your colleagues read your work.' And they did the same thing with their telementors, the people from the outside who 'stopped in' to read their work. Now, instead of one teacher to seventy students, some students had as many as ten telementors critiquing their writing.

"You see, when you make education public, you involve the community. You know, 'It takes a village to raise an educated child.' Well, if you have concerned parents who want to get involved, there's the way, right there on the Internet. What I'm doing as a teacher is providing to the world, to the community, the work we're doing in class."

Because Nellen has seen the immeasurable value of websites in his class and in the classes of others—the CyberEnglish page includes links to the Web pages of dozens of English teachers—he gets frustrated by those who seem to obstruct the shift away from the traditional classroom and toward a student-centered, technology-rich environment.

"Traditional education is 'one-way.' It's textbook to student, video to student, radio to student. What the Web does in terms of interaction is provide the student *choices*. Now it's 'two-way.' I can't direct the order the student wants to go in. He or she decides where to go. The Web allows for different kinds of learning."

And it isn't just the advanced students who benefit from technology, Nellen said.

"The AP kids, they're going to do okay in the traditional classroom because they're verbal," he explained. "But my classes have the special-ed kids, the bilingual learners, the visual learners . . . and what the Web does is provide access to the world so that my kids can *fly*. My hearing-impaired kids can read the text. I've had several quadriplegic students, and they can navigate their own way around the Web. My resource kids can take their time. They can spend a half an hour on a concept until they've got it."

The advantages of a class website even extend into the areas of assessment that have been thrust upon schools lately, Nellen explained.

"My kids pass those dreaded tests," he said. "And their attendance is great. Look, the computer is an enabling machine. People say it's not a panacea for education, but it *is* a panacea. It *can* work if it's done correctly. It approaches Dewey's 'learning by doing' and Gardner's eight intelligences. This one machine allows for *all* of that."

10

Now Presenting! PowerPoint and Beyond

With so much information available at the click of a mouse, many English teachers now complain that students cut and paste their way through assignments, downloading page after page of information without internalizing meaning. Requiring students to present ideas, with the help of software such as PowerPoint, authenticates learning and offers learners the opportunity to express their ideas through multimedia.

What Did You Learn? Using Presentations to Demonstrate Knowledge

One way to assess whether students have internalized meaning in any unit of study is to ask them to present their learning to their peers. Of course, those of us who have taught public speaking know how difficult it is to get some students up in front of the class. But unlike traditional "oral presentations," when students demonstrate learning with software such as PowerPoint, class attention moves away from the speaker and onto the screen. Consequently, those students who wouldn't be caught dead giving a formal speech can be successful presenting information to their peers. Using presentation software means that they aren't the subjects of scrutiny; their work is.

Furthermore, the multimedia aspects of presentation software engage students in ways traditional print seems to be unable to. The blending of text, sounds, images, and motion contribute to an overall effect that stimulates multiple intelligences and seems to engage learners.

Most important, students must master a number of interrelated skills in order to present information clearly and with appropriate media support. These skills build on those addressed in English classrooms every day: collaboration, problem solving, writing, reading, speaking, and listening.

According to Brunner and Tally, when students in language-arts classes participate in multimedia projects, they practice and develop complex thinking skills, communication and presentation skills, work management and interpersonal skills, and design and production skills (1999). The authors also argue that "students have far higher and more genuine standards for evaluating multimedia productions . . . than they do for the kind of written 'memos' they have traditionally been asked to produce for an audience of one—their teacher." In other words, using multimedia as a tool to demonstrate knowledge contributes to a learning-rich classroom.

Furthermore, if English teachers also teach some basic elements of design and visual literacy, then students can blend new knowledge about the media with new knowledge in the content area. As they *apply* what they know, students can begin to see the relevance of lessons learned in English classes.

Project Ideas: Keep It Real

Again, many language-arts teachers rely on student presentations to assess student knowledge of content. They want to make sure students don't just go online and download page after page of information. The purpose of many presentations is to ascertain what a student actually *knows*. With that in mind, consider some of the following project ideas.

- **The story synopsis**   A common presentation project asks students to highlight the major elements of a story: plot, characterization, setting, tone, theme. . . . Often students download clip art or pictures that illustrate some aspect of the literature. For example, if a student were doing a multimedia story synopsis of *The Scarlet Letter*, he or she might download photographs from the Demi Moore movie, a portrait of Nathaniel Hawthorne, examples of Puritan dress, and a map of New England. The student would need to explain, orally, the *relevance* of each of these items to the story.

- **The personal response to literature**   More and more, teachers are asking students to keep electronic journals, and a popular use of the e-journal is to ask students to share, with peers, personal responses to literature. Electronic journals in programs such as PowerPoint often include original narration and downloaded music. In preparing personal responses, students need to communicate their emotional reactions to a story; in so doing they communicate an understanding of the work. For instance, a student's personal response to Robert Cormier's *The Chocolate War* might include a memory about a time he or she stood up against a crowd—and lost. Further, the student can include hyperlinks to places that relate to the memory. In reviewing personal responses, the teacher generally looks for connections to the literature. The screen in Figure 10–1 shows what an e-journal response to *The Chocolate War* might look like.
- **The hypertext research project**   A typical English project involves having groups of students research a literary period or style. A PowerPoint presentation lends itself to the sharing of what students subsequently discover. Be sure students include links to the sites where they retrieved their information. That way, you can make sure they didn't copy the text word for word. Figure 10–2 shows what a screen from a hypertext research project might look like.

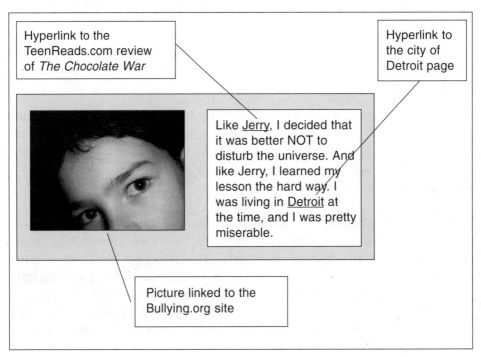

Hyperlink to the TeenReads.com review of *The Chocolate War*

Hyperlink to the city of Detroit page

Like Jerry, I decided that it was better NOT to disturb the universe. And like Jerry, I learned my lesson the hard way. I was living in Detroit at the time, and I was pretty miserable.

Picture linked to the Bullying.org site

Figure 10–1

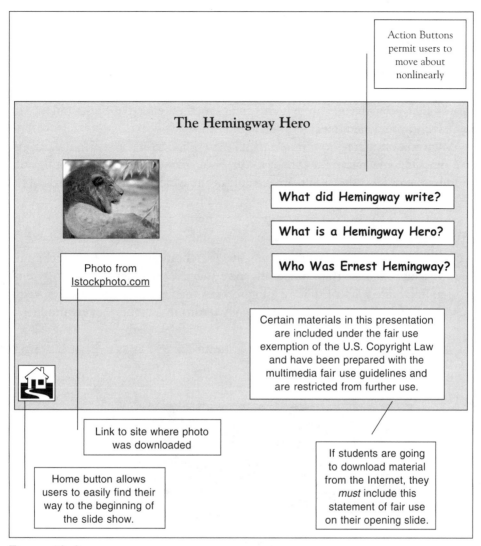

Figure 10–2

PowerWhat?

PowerPoint and other presentation packages such as Lotus' Freelance Graphics offer eye-catching ways to present information. Imagine the text capabilities of an overhead transparency combined with the visual appeal of a slide show, and you've got PowerPoint. Well, actually, it's much more than that. You can make text appear and disappear at the click of a mouse (no more blue fingers from wiping the marker off a transparency). You can have photos fade in and fade out. You can even add sound, music, and video to enhance the meaning of your presentation and to engage image-savvy students.

Most new computers come bundled with software—Microsoft Office or Lotus SmartSuite, for example—that includes a presentation package. If you're completely new to presentation software, consider working through the tutorials. Just click on Help, and key in *tutorial*, or go to this book's companion website for links to tutorials created specifically for educators. You can also work through the wizards that prompt you through the creation of an effective presentation. (In PowerPoint, you would select "AutoContent Wizard.")

Microsoft offers free PowerPoint templates for educators on its Digital Gallery Live site. Go to dgl.microsoft.com or to this book's companion website for the latest link. Figure 10–3 shows you an example of the education templates available.

Setting It Up: Flowcharts

Because so many students do multimedia presentations now, they might not think twice about how they should organize them. Consequently, they may end up spending quite a bit of time redoing screens they are unhappy with. As with most things, a little upfront planning usually results in a higher-quality product.

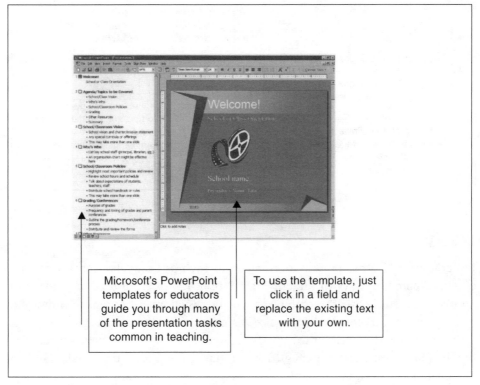

Figure 10–3

Have your students begin organizing their presentations by creating a flowchart. The most important aspect of the flowchart is to outline hierarchies. Important information should appear early in the presentation, and supporting information should follow. (Notice the connection to essay writing?)

Figure 10–4 shows a flowchart for a nonlinear presentation.

Designing the Presentation: Some Tips for Layout

No one expects English teachers to know everything there is to know about graphic design. But if you're familiar with a few "tricks of the trade," then you can help your students create powerful and effective presentations.

Many classroom presentations are done in a lab where a computer is connected to a special projector that casts the image onto a large screen. Other classroom presentations are done on SmartBoards, interactive white boards, or even on television monitors connected to a computer. On occasion, students will gather around a classroom computer to watch a classmate's presentation.

To ensure that your students' presentations are effective, however they are displayed, review the following points with your students.

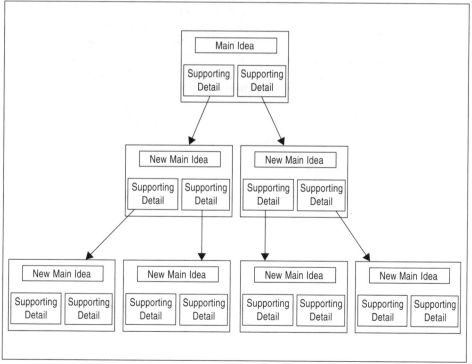

Figure 10–4

- **Typography**   Type can be a very powerful tool in communication. Different typefaces have different connotations. For example, the font called Script MT Bold suggests formality, whereas the font called Salvaged suggests, well, something that's been salvaged. Students should be sure their choice of typeface complements the message of the text. Furthermore, students should choose a point size that is large enough for people to read easily. Squinting at a computer screen causes eyestrain, not to mention irritability. Also, it's a good idea to stick with sans serif fonts for most computer documents. They tend to look cleaner—less cluttered—on the screen. For an example of serif and sans serif fonts, see Figure 10–5.
- **Color**   Using color purposefully can help students cue their audience into what's important. Text that contrasts sharply with its background (black on yellow, for example) signifies weighty information. Conversely, text that complements its background (black on gray) tends to be better for longer chunks of information. Your students might be interested to know that quite a bit of research has been done on the psychological effects of color. For example, it has been suggested that red suggests rage, whereas blue suggests serenity (Lohr 2003, 146).

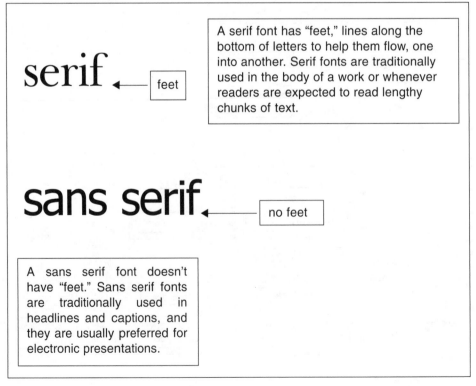

Figure 10–5

- **Chunking**   If your students remember only one design tip, it should be this one: do not fill your screens with text. If you've ever been forced to sit through a PowerPoint presentation that was nothing but screen after screen of text, you know how tedious it becomes. People don't read text on the screen the same way they read words in a book—which is why e-books have yet to take off. When people look at a computer screen, they tend to scan the whole thing, looking for key information. Instruct students to group, or chunk, bits of information together. Figure 10–6 shows a screen filled to overflowing with text and one that makes good use of chunking. Which would you rather read on a computer screen?

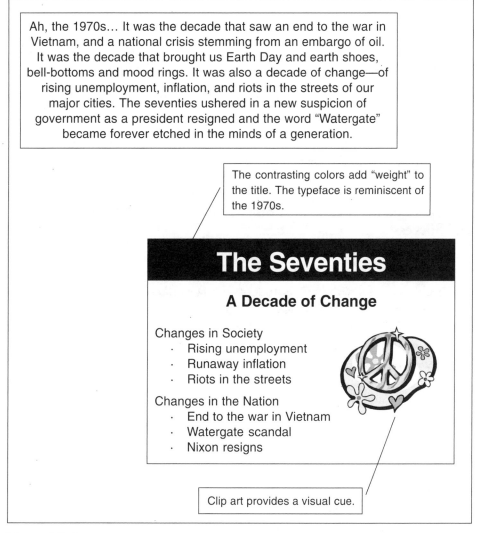

Figure 10–6

Assessing Levels of Learning: Asking Students to Reflect

We can learn a great deal about what students have actually learned by asking them to reflect on their work. Also, asking students to analyze their thought processes contributes to metacognition. Adapt the form in Figure 10–7 to meet the needs of your students. You can download a printable form by accessing the companion website.

Copyright Notice

Students who download material from the Internet for educational projects are exempted from copyright restrictions if they include the following statement at the *beginning* of their multimedia projects:

> Certain materials in this presentation are included under the fair use exemption of the U.S. Copyright Law and have been prepared with the multimedia fair use guidelines and are restricted from further use.

For more on the fair use exemption clause of the U.S. Copyright Law, visit the Library of Congress Copyright Site.

Students Sharing Meaning: A Story of Collaboration, Learning, and Success

Richard Williams is the ninth-grade English teacher in Alpharetta, Georgia, who shared some ideas about using word-processing software in Chapter 6. He has also been successful with having students use PowerPoint.

"I've always tried to encourage kids to put the meaning of literature into their own words," Williams began. "But I've found that PowerPoint really raises the bar."

Last semester, he asked his students to create "reinterpretations" of stories, novels, and plays studied in class using multimedia.

"What I was wanted for them was to reinterpret key aspects of the stories," he explained, "and then tell the story again, using lots of images, as if it were restaged. The goal was *not* to keep the images and concepts the same; I told them to monkey around a bit."

By asking them to place themes and plots in different contexts, Williams hoped his students would begin to recognize the universality and timelessness of literature. Further, he wanted them to internalize the stories being studied by building connections to people and images they were already familiar with. He knew he could determine how successful they were by analyzing their presentations.

Multimedia Project: Self-Reflection

1. What was the goal of your project? Do you think it achieved its goal?

2. What concepts from class did you include?

3. Did you find the flowcharting stage helpful or distracting? Why?

4. How long did you spend planning this project? How long did you spend creating this project? How long did you spend revising this project?

5. How did you select the information to include?

6. What resources did you use?

7. How did you decide which media to include?

8. In your opinion, how did the media contribute to the project's message?

9. What did you learn as a result of this project?

10. If you were to do a similar project in the future, what would you differently?

Figure 10–7

"First of all," Williams said, "when we start talking about these stories, especially Shakespeare, it's hard for the kids to connect. We were studying *A Midsummer Night's Dream*, and I asked the kids, who does Hermia remind you of? They immediately said Britney Spears. That got me thinking: What if the kids rewrote the story using Britney Spears and Justin Timberlake? And where PowerPoint is really valuable is that it really helps the kids build lasting connections because they're using images they find and download off the Internet."

In the PowerPoint presentations the students create, the sky is the limit, but they must be able to justify their choice of images.

"For example," Williams said, "in *Midsummer Night's Dream*, there's this huge theme of competition. So some of my guys restaged it in their multimedia presentation as a sumo wrestling match. They demonstrated that they understood what was going on, and they built a unique connection. And they really begin to make the right connections between the characters from the perspective of the images they select."

And, frankly, the technology itself is engaging, Williams said.

"I think the kids really like using it," he explained. "They especially like the new PowerPoint that runs on Windows XP. It's almost like a television studio. There's this whole concept of moving images and animation. . . . That really gets them involved. It's as if they are staging their own version of the play, and they feel they are in control. It gives them such a sense of freedom.

"You know, they can download music and sound effects, too. All together, the media elements help them to *visualize* what they are doing. And it's such an easy program. There are just so many things we can do with it."

In addition to building connections to the literature, creating multimedia presentations also helps to build writing skills and an understanding of voice and point of view.

"One of them, writing from the point of view of Hermia, said something like, 'No wonder he dumped you!' They become a part of the story; they take part in writing the text. They're joining their voices to Shakespeare's."

When it comes to navigating their way around PowerPoint and the Internet, students haven't needed a lot of teaching.

"I've had to teach them a few things," he said. "But the kids in this area are fairly savvy with computers. In fact, many of their parents work in the computer industry. They know this stuff. Now, they don't necessarily all know how to do everything in PowerPoint, but the general keyboarding skills transfer quickly. And they know the basics, like how to copy and paste, and they are familiar with the Internet."

Key to the success of the multimedia project, Williams believes, is its collaborative structure.

"The kids work in groups," he said. "One kid teaches another. I really don't have to do much; they pick it up really quick."

After the projects were completed, the students had a presentation day.

"We presented them two days before the final exam," Williams explained. "It was a really good review. Each group of students presented their rationales and gave some background, and then they set the PowerPoint slides to run automatically. Everyone in the class rated them and turned in a written evaluation."

The project isn't without the normal complications, however.

"Of course, our time is limited," Williams said. "And our access to the computer lab is also limited. We have several labs at our school, but there are so many people who want to use them. When we go, we have to go to do something really specific . . . like download clip art. I really like having the students use clip art. They work with visual representations, symbolic representations, not direct statements."

Williams is proud of the work his students produced, and he knows that they will remember the characters and plots of the stories they have read in class because they have created a personal connection to the literature; as with all the technology-based projects described in this book, they have participated in making their own meaning.

"The project was a real hit," he said. "They worked so hard on it. And anytime kids are working hard on a Shakespeare project, well. . . . Bottom line: They loved it. And they learned so much."

Works Cited

Beers, Kylene. 2002. *When Kids Can't Read: What Teachers Can Do*. Portsmouth, NH: Heinemann.

Brunner, Cornelia and William Tally. 1999. *The New Media Literacy Handbook*. NY: Anchor Books, Doubleday.

Burke, Jim. 2002. *Tools for Thought*. Portsmouth, NH: Heinemann.

Fish, Rich. 1999. "Audio Theater at the Millennium: Is There Really a Market for This Stuff?" [online]. Available from World Wide Web: (http://www.radiocollege.org/rc/rt2.html)

Gerbner, George. 1993. "Society's Storyteller: How TV Creates the Myths by Which We Live" [online]. Available from World Wide Web: (http://www.medialit.org/reading_room/article439.html)

Hesse, Karen. 1999. *Out of the Dust*. NY: Scholastic.

Lohr, Linda. 2003. *Creating Graphics for Learning and Performance: Lessons in Visual Literacy*. Upper Saddle River, NJ: Merrill.

Marzano, Robert, Barbara Gaddy and Ceri Dean. 2000. *What Works In Classroom Instruction*. Aurora, CO: Mid-continent Research for Education and Learning.

Owston, Ronald. 1997. "The World Wide Web: A Technology to Enhance Teaching and Learning?" *Educational Researcher* 26, no. 2 (March): 27–33.

Simkins, Michael, Karen Cole, Fern Tavalin, and Barbara Means. 2002. *Increasing Student Learning Through Multimedia Projects*. Alexandria, VA: Association for Supervision and Curriculum Development.

Steinbeck, John. 1939, 2002. *The Grapes of Wrath*. NY: Penguin.

Strommen, Erik. 1992. "Constructivism, Technology, and the Future of Classroom Learning" [online]. Available from World Wide Web: (http://www.ilt.columbia.edu/ilt/papers/construct.html)

Wright, Gary and Sherman Ross. 1994. "What is Black and White and Read All Over? The Funnies!" *Reading Improvement* 31, no. 1: 37–48.

Yoder, Maureen. 1999. "The Student WebQuest." *Learning and Leading with Technology* 26, no. 7 (April): 6–9, 52–53.